THY
WILL
BE DONE

THY
WILL
BE DONE

The Ten Commandments
❧ and the ❧
Christian Life

Gilbert Meilaender

B
Baker Academic
a division of Baker Publishing Group
Grand Rapids, Michigan

© 2020 by Gilbert Meilaender

Published by Baker Academic
a division of Baker Publishing Group
PO Box 6287, Grand Rapids, MI 49516-6287
www.bakeracademic.com

Printed in the United States of America

Library of Congress Cataloging-in-Publication Data
Names: Meilaender, Gilbert, 1946– author.
Title: Thy will be done : the Ten Commandments and the Christian life / Gilbert Meilaender.
Description: Grand Rapids : Baker Academic, a division of Baker Publishing Group, 2020. | Includes index.
Identifiers: LCCN 2019031833 | ISBN 9781540961969 (cloth)
Subjects: LCSH: Ten commandments—Criticism, interpretation, etc. | Christian life—Biblical teaching.
Classification: LCC BV4655 .M4344 2020 | DDC 241.5/2—dc23
LC record available at https://lccn.loc.gov/2019031833

Scripture quotations are from the Revised Standard Version of the Bible, copyright 1946, 1952 [2nd edition, 1971] National Council of the Churches of Christ in the United States of America. Used by permission. All rights reserved worldwide.

20 21 22 23 24 25 26   7 6 5 4 3 2 1

Contents

TO JUDY
As Always

Preface

In the pages that follow I do not aim at anything especially creative. Instead, I simply want to do what Christians have done many times before—namely, think about the Christian life in terms of the Ten Commandments, the Decalogue. As John Calvin says in the *Institutes*, the purpose of the Decalogue is that we may "express the image of God" in our lives.[1] To think through the shape of such a life is my aim in what follows.

To be sure, the Bible does not exactly contain a list of "ten commandments." The commandments appear as an unnumbered list in chapter 20 of Exodus and chapter 5 of Deuteronomy, and the account in Exodus begins with the simple statement, "God spoke all these words." Yet, for centuries not only Christians but also Jews have numbered the commandments as ten. More exactly we may speak of the "ten words" (which in Greek became *deka logous*, and in English "Decalogue"). Because God is said to have written these ten words on two stone tablets, it has also been common to divide them into "two tables"—the

1. John Calvin, *Institutes of the Christian Religion*, ed. John T. McNeill, trans. Ford Lewis Battles, Library of Christian Classics 20 (Philadelphia: Westminster, 1960), 2.8.51. All quotations from the *Institutes* are from this translation.

first treating our relation to God, the second our relation to one another. Useful as that division can be in certain respects, my own discussion draws the second and third commandments into close connection with the bonds of community to which the commandments of the second table point.

While it has been common to number the commandments as ten, the precise way of numbering them varies. I doubt whether there is any way to demonstrate that one numbering must be preferred to another. I will follow the numbering that has been used by Roman Catholics and Lutherans. For this approach the first table consists of three commandments—to have no other gods, not to use God's name in vain, and to sanctify the holy day. The second table then enjoins honoring one's father and mother and prohibits unjustified killing, adultery, theft, false testimony, and coveting (first of the neighbor's house; then of the neighbor's wife, servants, or possessions).

The principal Christian alternative to this numbering is that used by the Eastern Orthodox churches and many Protestant bodies. That alternative treats the prohibition of graven images, which is not an independently numbered commandment for Roman Catholics and Lutherans, as the second commandment— giving four commandments in the first table. If the total number is still to be ten, the second table must be compressed into six commandments. The Orthodox and many Protestants accomplish this by combining the commandments that forbid coveting into one, whereas they remain separate (as the ninth and tenth) in the Roman Catholic and Lutheran Decalogue. The traditional Jewish numbering provides yet a third alternative, which is distinguished chiefly by the fact that the prologue, which identifies the One who gives these commands as the God who brought Israel out of Egypt, is numbered as the first commandment.

Not a lot hangs on this for me since, as will eventually be apparent, I treat the seventh, ninth, and tenth commandments together as aspects of what I will call the "possessions bond." More generally, I use all the commandments after the first as an invitation to reflect upon the importance of five different bonds that unite human beings in community: the marriage bond, the family bond, the life bond, the possessions bond, and the speech bond.

Clearly, however, the first commandment does have a special place. Quite rightly, therefore, Martin Luther emphasized the manner in which all other commandments relate to the first. To have no other gods—to love and trust God above all else—enables a person to keep the other commandments. And something like the reverse may also be true. For it is in and through the various bonds connecting human lives that God works on us, beginning to make of us people who can love him with the whole of our heart, soul, strength, and mind.

Nevertheless, the connection between the first commandment and the others can also create difficulties for the Christian life. There is tension between the first commandment and the bonds of life to which the other commandments point. How exactly shall we reconcile the requirement that we love God wholly and above all else with the fact that our hearts are rightly given in love to others and other good things within the five bonds of human life? This creates tension within the Christian life and points to an enduring problem for Christian thought.

The commandments are, I think, best thought of within the full sweep of the biblical story. Thus, in the massive and never-completed volumes of his *Church Dogmatics*, Karl Barth envisions ethics as offering an account of human action that corresponds to the threefold form of God's action in creation, reconciliation, and redemption.[2] Because we are God's creatures,

2. Barth himself provides a succinct description of his approach in three places: (1) *Church Dogmatics* II/2, 549–50; (2) *Church Dogmatics* III/4, 24–26; and (3) pp.

there must be some account that accepts, honors, and celebrates distinctively human agency. Because we are sinners whose lives are disordered and in need of healing, God has in Jesus acted to reconcile us to himself. And because we are heirs of the future God has promised, we will one day be perfected in a way that does not obliterate our created humanity but, rather, expresses God's faithfulness to it.

Without attempting in any way to do justice to the richness of Barth's lavishly developed structure, I suggest that Christian reflection on the moral instruction in the Decalogue cannot ignore any of these angles of vision if we truly want to pray, "Thy will be done." The three angles of vision do not simply follow one another in lockstep sequence, nor does any one of them ever replace another. But even if it is difficult to combine the three, it is still important, as Barth put it, to recall that in ethics our task is "to accompany this history of God and man from creation to reconciliation and redemption, indicating the mystery of the encounter at each point on the path according to its own distinctive character."[3] Not without good reason, therefore, did Luther write in the Preface to his Large Catechism, "This much is certain: those who know the Ten Commandments perfectly know the entire Scriptures."[4]

6–11 of *The Christian Life*, a fragment of the unfinished discussion of the ethics of reconciliation in *Church Dogmatics* IV.

3. Karl Barth, *Church Dogmatics* III/4, ed. G. W. Bromiley and T. F. Torrance, trans. A. T. Mackay et al. (Edinburgh: T&T Clark, 1961), 26.

4. Robert Kolb and Timothy J. Wengert, eds., *The Book of Concord: The Confessions of the Evangelical Lutheran Church* (Minneapolis: Fortress, 2000), 382.

❧ CHAPTER 1 ❧

The Law of Christ

The Church lives by the "fathers" of Israel, by the fellowship
of the spirit with Abraham, Isaac and Jacob, Moses, David
and Elijah. . . . These fathers of Israel, and they alone, ought
in strict justice to be called the "fathers of the Church."

Karl Barth[1]

It is obvious that the Decalogue has played a central role in the
church's understanding of how Christians should live. In their
confessions, in their preaching, and perhaps especially in their
catechetical instruction, churches have used the Decalogue as
a framework for understanding the will of God for our lives.
Jesus himself seems to regard the commandments of the Decalogue as an articulation of the goodness God requires (e.g.,
Luke 18:18–20). And in Galatians (5:14) St. Paul draws these

This chapter is a revised version of the article "The Decalogue as the Law of
Christ," which appeared in *Pro Ecclesia* 27, no. 3 (2018): 338–49. Used with
permission.

1. Karl Barth, *Church Dogmatics* II/2, ed. G. W. Bromiley and T. F. Torrance,
trans. G. W. Bromiley (Edinburgh: T&T Clark, 1957), 204.

"ten words" into one, writing, "The whole law is fulfilled in
one word, 'You shall love your neighbor as yourself.'" A similar
passage in Romans (13:8–10) indicates clearly that the commandments Paul is drawing together in this one are those of
the Decalogue.[2] Would, however, that things were really this
clear and simple. Readers of St. Paul will know better than to
suppose that they are.

The Problem

St. Paul seems to hold two seemingly incompatible beliefs—that
Christians ought to obey the law's moral demands *and* that the
time of the law ended with the coming of Christ. The same
apostle who characterizes the content of neighbor-love in terms
of the commandments of the Decalogue can also write that those
who live in Christ have "died to the law" and are "discharged"
from its demands (Rom. 7:4–6). We should therefore not be surprised that Christians have disagreed—sometimes vehemently—
about what role the moral law should play in their lives. Although
we often suppose that we can find the solution to this question
in the writings of St. Paul, perhaps it is better to think of him
as setting for us the terms of a problem that we must sort out
for ourselves.

One very common—and by no means foolish or obviously
mistaken—attempt to solve this problem has been to distinguish

2. "Owe no one anything, except to love one another; for he who loves his
neighbor has fulfilled the law. The commandments, 'You shall not commit adultery, You shall not kill, You shall not steal, You shall not covet,' and any other
commandment, are summed up in this sentence, 'You shall love your neighbor as
yourself.' Love does no wrong to a neighbor; therefore love is the fulfilling of the
law." We may wonder whether this does not overlook the very different "words"
traditionally understood as the "first table" of the law—words that treat our relation not to our "neighbors" but to God. I set this question aside for the moment
and will eventually return to it.

several different kinds of law found in the Old Testament. First, there is the sort of law we call "moral," of which the Decalogue is the foremost example. Although the Decalogue is not the only example of moral law in the Old Testament, it clearly occupies a special place, making it unsurprising that Christians have so often taken it as a pattern for instruction in the moral life.[3] The special place of the Decalogue can be seen in the fact that it is spoken to the people of Israel directly by God, not mediated through Moses. And, as has often been noted, its commands are apodictic. That is, they are expressed as short prohibitions, seemingly universal in scope. Rather than being the sort of case law intended to govern the political life of a community, they seem to express standards of behavior or conditions of association that apply to all human beings and societies (past, present, and future). Though often disobeyed, these commandments outline a widely held sense of decent behavior. This does not mean that we always govern our behavior in accord with these laws. It just means that, as C. S. Lewis put it, "the moment anyone tells me I am not keeping it, there starts up in my mind a string of excuses."[4]

In addition to moral law, Old Testament legislation includes laws intended to govern both Israel's political life and its cultic life. Examples of the first include laws related to conditions of servitude, cities of refuge, war, and testimony in legal cases.

---

3. The Decalogue is by no means the only part of Old Testament legislation that has the look of moral law. Many of the prohibitions of the "Holiness Code" in Leviticus—in chaps. 17 and 18, for example—enunciate requirements similar to those of the Decalogue and seem to apply not only to Israelites but also to "sojourners" living with them. However, the "ten words" also occupied a special place in early Judaism. Until the second century after Christ they were read regularly in the synagogue. But, writes Robert M. Grant, "Jewish enthusiasm for the Decalogue diminished as a result of Christian use in the second century, and it was withdrawn from the synagogue liturgy" ("The Decalogue in Early Christianity," *Harvard Theological Review* 40 [January 1947]: 2).

4. C. S. Lewis, *Mere Christianity* (New York: Macmillan, 1960), 6.

Examples of the second include required sacrifices, dietary laws, and the ritual for the Day of Atonement. Among such cultic or ceremonial laws are requirements connected with keeping the Sabbath. The fact that this cultic law of the Sabbath occupies an important place in the Decalogue constitutes a special problem that will eventually require our attention.

When Christians have distinguished these three sorts of law from one another, the point has often been to suggest that when St. Paul writes, "Christ is the end of the law" (Rom. 10:4), he refers to the political and cultic laws of the Old Testament but not to the moral law. Hence, on this view, the requirements of the Decalogue—being moral law—would have continuing validity for all people, Christians among them. As I noted above, this is not an obviously mistaken approach, and in fact it may be the best we can do to bring order to St. Paul's various discussions of the law. We have to grant, however, that it does not work perfectly. Sometimes Paul does not seem to distinguish various kinds of law within Israel's Torah. Thus, for example, he writes in Galatians 5:3, "I testify again to every man who receives circumcision that he is bound to keep the whole law." But elsewhere, when he refers to the law—as, for example, in Romans 2:14–16—he quite clearly is thinking of moral law rather than Old Testament legislation as a whole. So I return to what I said earlier: St. Paul sets for us the terms of the problem; to deal with it requires our own constructive thought.

Puzzling over Galatians

What is the relation between faith (*pistis*) and law (*nomos*) in the Christian life? Galatians offers us two different patterns of thought with which to think about this question. The discussion in 2:15–3:12 is dominated by a contrast between two different ways we might try to live before God. The contrast is not precisely between faith and law; rather, St. Paul contrasts a life of faith with a life based on "works of law." And the implication seems to be that, although faith cannot coexist with reliance on *works* of law, it is not opposed to the law as such.

We see this in the way Paul uses the story of Abraham in this part of Galatians. He writes that God "preached the gospel beforehand to Abraham" (3:8). That is, already long before the time of Christ two possibilities exist for Abraham. He can rely on works of law (which, clearly, would here not mean Old Testament law specifically), or he can live by faith. The contrast is not between two historical periods, one governed by law and the other by faith. Instead, the contrast is an existential one within the life of a person who in every moment stands before God, summoned to rely on the good news of the gospel rather than on "works of law." Thus, these verses do not say that the moral law has no place within the life of faith; they say that reliance on works of law is contrary to faith in the good news of God's grace. So this section of Galatians seems to contrast two different ways of life that are possibilities for anyone, anywhere, at any time—and it does not in any way suggest that the moral law has no place as instruction and guidance for one who lives by faith.

In Galatians 3:13–4:31 the emphasis shifts. Now the law seems to have its place in a time before Christ came. Moreover, the time after Christ came and the time of faith are almost indistinguishable (as in 3:23–26). In this section of Galatians, therefore, *pistis* and *nomos* are not contrasting bases for a person's life; rather, they mark a break in history between two different ways in which God acts. The time when Old Testament law governed—a time before "faith" came—was limited, and the law was a custodian put in place by God to accomplish certain purposes. But now that Christ has come (or, to say roughly the same thing, faith has come), believers are no longer confined under that custodian but are adopted children of God free from law, whose lives are governed by the Spirit of Christ.

How shall we hold together these two patterns of thought? Using the second pattern from Galatians, we could take as our starting point the idea that once Christ comes, the time of law is ended and the time of faith begun. Then, one might say, those who live by faith do not in any way govern or guide their lives by the law. Or we could take as our starting point the first pattern of thought—not, that is, a contrast between two historical periods (a time of law and a time of faith) but, instead, a contrast within any person's life between reliance on works of law and faith that simply trusts the gospel. Then, one might say, to live by faith is not to ignore or be uninstructed by the commands of the law. It simply means that we do not rely on obeying the law to make us right with God.

In short, Galatians leaves us not with an answer but with a puzzle we must sort out. In my judgment the first pattern of thought in Galatians is our best starting point. Believers are not to rely on works of law, nor to place their hope in obedience to the moral law; nevertheless, they are not free to set it aside or to imagine that, once Christ has come, it should no longer shape and direct their conduct. To suppose otherwise would be, as Helmut Thielicke put it, to think of the Christian life as an "abstraction"—a static condition rather than a "pilgrimage" empowered by grace.[5] Therefore, when in Romans 10:4 St. Paul writes that Christ is the "end" of the law, so that righteousness before God is available for anyone who believes, this is best taken to mean that Christ is the "goal" of the law, not

5. Helmut Thielicke, *Theological Ethics*, vol. 1, *Foundations* (Philadelphia: Fortress, 1966), 130. The term "pilgrimage" to describe the Christian life is on p. 132.

its "termination."[6] In God's gracious purpose the law points to Israel's Messiah, whose death and resurrection is the goal of Israel's life, shaped as it is by God's law.

Hence, the entire Old Testament law—moral, cultic, political—points toward the One who was to come. Some aspects of that law, although they no longer direct Christian conduct, served and serve as witness to the One who was to come. Other aspects of that law—in particular, those we call moral—continue to instruct us about what it means to follow Christ. It is the task of Christian moral reflection to distinguish within the law, all of which has its goal in Christ, what does and what does not continue to direct the life of believers within "the Israel of God" (Gal. 6:16).

Once we realize that St. Paul quite unselfconsciously sets side by side in Galatians these two ways of speaking about law, faith, gospel, and promise, we see that even a Pauline letter such as Galatians—with its ringing emphasis on Christian freedom—should not be understood as teaching that Christians are free to ignore the requirements of the moral law. In fact, St. Paul once described himself (1 Cor. 9:21) as *ennomos Christou*, "subject to the law of Christ"—a phrase characterized by Thielicke as "the most felicitous and precise designation imaginable" for depicting St. Paul's view that Christians, while not "under" the law, are nonetheless not "without" law toward God.[7] Nor is St. Paul's a special case. For as he says in Galatians, that great epistle of Christian freedom, when believers bear one another's burdens, they "fulfil the law of Christ" (6:2). They live in fellowship, as Barth says, with the fathers of Israel.[8]

---

6. For this reading I follow C. E. B. Cranfield's discussion in *A Critical and Exegetical Commentary on the Epistle to the Romans* (Edinburgh: T&T Clark, 1979), 2:515–20. This is probably a better reading of Rom. 10:4 than the reading I noted earlier, which interprets the verse to mean that Christ is the end (i.e., termination) of political and cultic, but not moral, law in the Old Testament.

7. Thielicke, *Theological Ethics*, 137.

8. Barth, *Church Dogmatics* II/2, 204.

The Decalogue as Christian Instruction

Reading Galatians in this way is advantageous in several respects. It keeps us from supposing that, in order to take St. Paul seriously, we must separate Christ from God's calling of Israel as his holy, elect people. For example, it allows and invites us to take seriously the Psalms as the church's prayer book, to pray them along with Jesus, the faithful Israelite. We can say that the precepts of the LORD rejoice the heart (Ps. 19:8); we can believe that one who delights in and meditates on the law of the LORD day and night will be blessed (1:1–2); we can pray that the LORD would make us know his ways and teach us his paths (25:4); we can give thanks that God's word is a lamp to our feet and a light to our path (119:105). And it means that we need not set St. Paul over against New Testament passages such as 1 John 5:3: "This is the love of God, that we keep his commandments. And his commandments are not burdensome."

The commandments that have Israel's Messiah as their goal become for Christians instruction in "the law of Christ," and the Decalogue gives direction and shape to their lives. On the one hand, the whole law is fulfilled in the command to love one's neighbor. But, on the other hand, the various commands of the Decalogue are needed to give specificity to the meaning of this neighbor-love. To suppose that we could "just make do with the general commandment to love" would, as C. E. B. Cranfield writes, "be altogether mistaken. For, while we most certainly need the summary to save us from missing the wood for the trees and from understanding the particular commandments in a rigid, literalistic, unimaginative, pedantic, or loveless way, we are equally in need of the particular commandments into which the law breaks down the general obligation of love, to save us from resting content with vague, and often hypocritical, sentiments, which . . . we are all prone to mistake for Christian love."[9] Thus, we should not picture the commands of the second table as simply an addition or supplement to those of the first. On the contrary, they specify what it means to have no other God than Israel's Lord. They offer an "exposition" of the first table "from the standpoint of the plurality of life's relationships"— depicting "the actualization of the First Commandment in the various relationships of life."[10]

Thus, it is fitting that the commandments of the Decalogue should become useful for—indeed, central to—the church's catechetical instruction. In this context the commandments are not an external law imposed upon recalcitrant subjects; rather, they give shape to the life directed by the Spirit of Christ. It is, as Bonhoeffer writes, "grace to know God's commands. They free us from self-made plans and conflicts. They make our steps certain and our way joyful."[11]

Luther's Small and Large Catechisms offer a striking example of a catechetical use of the Decalogue.[12] It is striking especially because there are aspects of Luther's theology that might seem to leave little place for this kind of instruction in the Christian life. Indeed, the tensions within Luther's writings about the moral life are palpable. On the one hand, he finds in the commandments instruction about the sort of life that pleases God. Thus, he writes in the Large Catechism: "Here, then, we have the Ten Commandments, a summary of divine teaching on what we are to do to make our whole life pleasing to God. They are the true fountain from which all good works

9. Cranfield, *Epistle to the Romans*, 2:679.

10. Thielicke, *Theological Ethics*, 138.

11. Dietrich Bonhoeffer, *"Life Together" and "Prayerbook of the Bible,"* ed. Geffrey B. Kelly, trans. James H. Burtness, Dietrich Bonhoeffer Works 5 (Minneapolis: Fortress, 1996), 164.

12. I will use the texts as translated in Robert Kolb and Timothy J. Wengert, eds., *The Book of Concord: The Confessions of the Evangelical Lutheran Church* (Minneapolis: Fortress, 2000).

must spring, the true channel through which all good works must flow."[13]

On the other hand, in writings other than the catechisms Luther sometimes seems to set aside such moral instruction as irrelevant to the life of faith. He manages this with two quick moves. First, he characterizes the Old Testament legislation—including the Decalogue—as law "given only to the people of Israel" and, hence, "no longer binding on us."[14] Even the Decalogue governs Christian conduct only insofar as it happens to coincide with the natural law, which, according to St. Paul (in Rom. 2), is written on human hearts. Then a second move seems to dispense even with the natural law as instruction for Christians. For it is abolished "through faith spiritually, which is nothing else than the fulfilling of the law."[15] Hence, "if every man had faith we would need no more laws. Everyone would of himself do good works all the time, as his faith shows him."[16]

Clearly, this depiction of the Christian life is not complex enough to account for Luther's own use of the Decalogue, especially in his catechisms. To say only that love fulfills the law misses the point I quoted from Cranfield earlier—namely, that we need "the particular commandments into which the law breaks

13. Kolb and Wengert, *Book of Concord*, 428.

14. Martin Luther, "How Christians Should Regard Moses," *Luther's Works* (Philadelphia: Fortress, 1960), 35:164. The evidence for this, according to Luther, is that the Decalogue begins by identifying God as the One who brought Israel out of Egypt. Therefore, he writes, "this text makes it clear that even the Ten Commandments do not pertain to us. For God never led us out of Egypt, but only the Jews" (p. 165). But this hardly does justice to the way the New Testament understands that exodus from Egypt. Matthew (2:15) sees Jesus as the faithful Israelite, called out of Egypt by Israel's Lord. Indeed, the entire second chapter of Matthew's Gospel points back to the exodus, and it is impossible to understand the significance of Jesus and the community of his followers if his story is not read in at least some continuity with that of Israel.

15. Martin Luther, "Against the Heavenly Prophets in the Matter of Images and Sacraments," *Luther's Works* (Philadelphia: Fortress, 1958), 40:97.

16. Martin Luther, "Treatise on Good Works," *Luther's Works* (Philadelphia: Fortress, 1966), 44:34–35.

down the general obligation of love, to save us from resting content with vague, and often hypocritical, sentiments, which . . . we are all prone to mistake for Christian love." One of the great strengths of Luther's catechisms is the way he ties each of the commandments to the first. When he asks what the first commandment, which forbids having other gods, means, Luther answers simply, "We are to fear, love, and trust God above all things."[17] Following that, his explanation of each of the other commandments begins by connecting its meaning to the first: "We are to fear and love God, so that . . ."

Powerful and insightful as this is, taken alone it may lead us to miss a distinction between the person and the works the person does. We can see this, for instance, when Luther writes that in the work of faith "all good works exist, and from faith these works receive a borrowed goodness."[18] This might too easily suggest that the only work God cares about is the work of faith, but if that were the case we would be hard-pressed to explain the attention Luther gives in his catechisms to the variety of ways in which we may help or harm others. Suppose a Christian man who has been grouchy and ill-tempered with his children tries hard to do better and succeeds at least in part. With that changed behavior God is well pleased, whatever we say about the state of the man's faith. His changed behavior is better—has its own goodness—not just in our eyes but also in God's.

To have faith—that is, to be a person who is at peace with God and who trusts that for Christ's sake God is not our enemy— does not efface the distinction between behavior that pleases or displeases God, that conforms to God's will or does not so conform. On the contrary, to have faith means that, rejoicing "in our hope of sharing the glory of God" (Rom. 5:2), we trust the

---

17. Kolb and Wengert, *Book of Concord*, 351.
18. Luther, "Treatise on Good Works," 24.

promise in the Decalogue's commands: You *shall* love the LORD your God with all your heart, soul, and mind. You *shall* love your neighbor as yourself. God will make us people who truly delight in and love his commands. Unless we say something like that, we will hardly know what to make of Luther's catechisms or how it can be that he writes at the close of his discussion of the Ten Commandments in the Large Catechism, "We should prize and value them above all other teachings as the greatest treasure God has given us."[19]

George Lindbeck once observed how essential it is to see Luther not only as "theological controversialist" but also—and even "primarily"—as "pastor and catechist."[20] In the controversies treated in the first sort of writings—of which there are, of course, many—Luther often underscores the theme that the Christian life is marked by freedom from the law, that law and gospel are simply and irrevocably antithetical. Not so, however, in works of the second sort—and, paradigmatically, in the Small and Large Catechisms. "In the Catechisms," Lindbeck notes, "the theological issues of justification by faith alone, of the total corruption of fallen human nature, of double predestination, and of the opposition between law and gospel are never mentioned *expressis verbis*."[21] Nor do the catechisms invite us to suppose that concern for morality is incompatible with Christian faith.

We should not be surprised, then, to find that in the Large Catechism Luther calls the Ten Commandments "a summary of divine teaching on what we are to do to make our whole life pleasing to God."[22] Moreover, on Luther's reading each of the commandments turns out to instruct us not only about behavior

19. Kolb and Wengert, *Book of Concord*, 431.
20. George Lindbeck, "Martin Luther and the Rabbinic Mind," in *Understanding the Rabbinic Mind: Essays on the Hermeneutic of Max Kadushin*, ed. Peter Ochs (Atlanta: Scholars Press, 1990), 141.
21. Lindbeck, "Martin Luther and the Rabbinic Mind," 143.
22. Kolb and Wengert, *Book of Concord*, 428.

that is forbidden but also, more positively, about how we are to foster the well-being of others in countless ways. To see this is to see why Luther's suggestion that the Decalogue governs the lives of Christians only insofar as it happens to coincide with the natural law does not actually account for his own explication of the commandments.

Consider, for example, several aspects of his treatment of the seventh commandment (forbidding stealing) in the Large Catechism. To some degree Luther does treat the prohibition as a kind of natural law, for he suggests that human life in society is hardly possible if this commandment is not at least generally observed. "Anyone who robs and takes things by violence and dishonesty must," he writes, "put up with someone else who plays the same game."[23] There is a kind of empirical, commonsense quality to such a statement, for no society can survive if it does not enable people to secure and protect the things they need to live.

It would be hard, however, to understand everything Luther says in his discussion of the seventh commandment as nothing more than an unfolding of the natural law. Beyond the obvious negative requirements that we not wrong others by taking or damaging their possessions, the commandment, on Luther's reading, requires that we "promote and further our neighbors' interests, and when they suffer any want, we are to help, share, and lend to both friends and foes."[24] This goes well beyond what a society needs simply to survive, and it clearly has been shaped by Jesus' own teaching in the Sermon on the Mount. And if we ask why Luther thinks we should treat others this way and why we are able to do so, it is evident that something more than natural law is at work. Grace turns out to have an important place not only in dogmatic theology but also in moral theology. "You have," he writes, "a rich Lord, who is surely sufficient for

23. Kolb and Wengert, *Book of Concord*, 419.
24. Kolb and Wengert, *Book of Concord*, 419–20.

your needs and will let you lack or want for nothing."[25] But one learns this not from nature but from "the law of Christ," which instructs us to "bear one another's burdens" (Gal. 6:2).

It may be helpful, therefore, to follow the suggestion of Christopher Seitz that for Christians the Decalogue is not simply natural law but is also God's gift to Israel, his elect people. And just as some (but only some) portions of Israel's law were also binding on "sojourners" living within Israel, so now Christians—incorporated into Christ, the faithful Israelite—also become "sojourners in the midst of Israel."[26] Something like that seems to be St. Paul's view when he writes to the mostly Gentile congregation in Corinth that "our fathers" were part of the covenant people who made the wilderness march from Egypt to the promised land (1 Cor. 10:1). And such an assumption must underlie his command that the Corinthians remove from their fellowship a man who is living with his father's wife (1 Cor. 5:1–2)—behavior that is specifically prohibited in Old Testament law which now, it seems, applies also to Gentiles who have been incorporated into the covenant people.[27] To hold in this way that some parts of Israel's law now also govern the lives of Gentiles who have become "sojourners in the midst of Israel" is not to say that the commandments of the second table should not also be seen as enunciating a natural law valid for all human beings (as St. Paul seems to think of it in the second chapter of Romans). Neither approach to the Decalogue need exclude the other.

In any case, those portions of Israel's law that are moral—not only the Decalogue but certainly the Decalogue—continue to specify for Christians the law of Christ, the will of God that

25. Kolb and Wengert, *Book of Concord*, 420.

26. Christopher R. Seitz, "The Ten Commandments: Positive and Natural Law and the Covenants Old and New—Christian Use of the Decalogue and Moral Law," in *I Am the Lord Your God: Christian Reflections on the Ten Commandments*, ed. Carl E. Braaten and Christopher R. Seitz (Grand Rapids: Eerdmans, 2005), 33.

27. See Lev. 18:8; Deut. 22:30; 27:20.

is to be done here on earth as it is in heaven. From yet another angle, then, we see that there was and is a kind of wisdom in the distinction between moral, cultic, and political legislation that governed the life of ancient Israel.

The Decalogue as Instructional Prophecy[28]

It is important for us to see, as the following chapters will assume, that living "under the law of Christ" is the way to freedom, to the future in which it will be evident that hidden in the commands is God's promise to make us holy. Here I offer a homely illustration of what this might mean.

The journalist Christopher Caldwell once wrote a short piece on "the management secrets of Bill Belichick," head coach of the New England Patriots in the National Football League.[29] Whatever one thinks of Belichick the person, there is no disputing the fact that he is a great—perhaps the greatest ever—professional football coach. Caldwell notes the oddity that some exceptional players seem not to fit into Belichick's system, while others who are less skilled excel with the Patriots. They develop that ability by drilling day in and day out, practicing how to react in a variety of game situations, so that eventually they can react as if by instinct. But, of course, it isn't instinct at all. It is the kind of freedom that comes from having entered fully into the structure and disciplines of the system.

Caldwell ends his short essay with just a few sentences that capture the Patriots' approach: "You follow rules to attain your

28. The idea of instructional prophecy is my appropriation of the concept of "parenetic prophecy" developed in Reinhard Hütter, "The Tongue—Fallen and Restored: Some Reflections on the Three Voices of the Eighth Commandment," in Braaten and Seitz, *I Am the Lord Your God*, 189–205.

29. Christopher Caldwell, "Pats' Solutions: The Management Secrets of Bill Belichick," *The Weekly Standard* 22, February 6, 2017, 16, 18.

freedom. You learn by rote so that you can live with abandonment. This, too, is a truth of wide application." What other
"applications" Caldwell may have had in mind, I do not know;
however, learning by rote in order to live with abandonment is
not a bad way to understand the place of the Decalogue in the
Christian life.

The particular commandments, both as Christian instruction and as natural law, function in three ways. They help us
to specify the meaning of the general obligation to love and to
bear one another's burdens. In doing so, of course, the same
commandments will often function in a second way—making
clear the disorder of our world and its need for healing. But the
commandments serve one further purpose, the most important,
since by God's grace we follow rules in order to attain freedom.
As instructional prophecy they "announce the future of the life
with God that has already become present in the life of faith."[30]
They make clear what the Spirit of Christ is doing—sometimes,
though not always, in hidden ways—in the lives of those who, as
St. Paul says, rejoice in the hope of "sharing the glory of God"
(Rom. 5:2).

30. Hütter, "The Tongue—Fallen and Restored," 201–2.

❧ CHAPTER 2 ❧

The Marriage Bond

You shall not commit adultery.

Exodus 20:14

Important as the bond of marriage is to human life, we should not forget that it is an expression—indeed, the central expression—of something more fundamental still: the creation of humanity as male and female. "God created man in his own image, in the image of God he created him; male and female he created them" (Gen. 1:27). We do not all marry, but we are all created as male or female. We might say that built into our created nature from the outset is a task—the task of learning to accept the fundamental difference between male and female and to live in harmonious community, the task of forming the human community in the image of the God who from eternity is not a solitary monad but a fellowship in love of Father, Son, and Spirit. Pope John Paul II made this point directly and simply in the 1981 Apostolic Exhortation *Familiaris Consortio*: "God is love and in Himself He lives a mystery of personal loving

communion. Creating the human race in His own image and
continually keeping it in being, God inscribed in the humanity
of man and woman the *vocation*, and thus the capacity and
responsibility, *of love* and communion."[1]

Beginning here, with our creation as male and female, is a reminder that—marked as we are by that sexual differentiation—the
body matters to a person's identity. That important truth is often
obscured in our world when the language of "sexual difference"
is regularly replaced by "gender difference." Sexual difference is
a bodily, biological category that is not culturally malleable in
the way gender distinctions (of masculinity and femininity) are.

Replacing the language of "sex" with that of "gender" does not
overcome the differences that sometimes cause conflict between
men and women. On the contrary, it is an attempt to escape the
task set before us in the creation. In so doing it loses the meaning of the body for personal identity. Choice then becomes the
primary determinant of who we are, and the moral significance
of our embodied condition is set aside. Christians should know
better, for we know the body as God's creation, as the place of
God's personal presence among us in Jesus, and as the body that
God will one day raise to share the new creation Jesus now lives.
Here, therefore, we will think of marriage as the central expression of our creation as male *and* female, male *or* female—people
made for community in love by the God who is love.

The Marriage Bond in Creation

In ordering our lives the Creator has made us needy beings,
dependent upon others, and the creation of humanity as male

---

1. *Familiaris Consortio* 11 (emphasis added). Available online at http://scborromeo
.org/docs/familaris_consortio.pdf.

and female is the most fundamental mark of that neediness. Marriage is, therefore, a good gift that comes to us from the hand of God. It is, of course, a limited good—limited, that is, by the course of earthly life, which always moves toward death. But even while acknowledging that limit, we can praise the Creator for the gift of marital love.

The commandment forbidding adultery, deepened by Jesus in the Sermon on the Mount to include even the thoughts and desires that might lead to adultery, exists to protect marriage as one of the fundamental bonds of human life. Although the sixth commandment does not specifically refer to sexual relations between those who are unmarried—to fornication rather than adultery—it is clear that, existing to protect marriage as it does, the commandment at least implicitly teaches that marriage is the context within which the sexual act is appropriate. Still, it is also true that adultery involves harms that fornication does not. As the biblical scholar Patrick Miller has noted, the aim of this commandment is not so much that I should protect my marriage as that I should protect my neighbor's. "All of the commandments in the second table are aimed at protecting the well-being of members of the community by placing upon each one a responsibility for the other/neighbor."[2] Thus, adultery, which breaks a promise solemnly made, is not just sexual sin; it has its roots in selfish desire. An adulterer now ignores those legitimate claims and treats both his spouse and the neighbor unjustly.

Moreover, the commandment's focus on adultery embeds our marriages within the biblical understanding of God's covenant with Israel. "Your Maker is your husband," Isaiah says to exiled Israel (54:5), assuring them that the God who covenanted with

2. Patrick D. Miller, *The Ten Commandments* (Louisville: Westminster John Knox, 2009), 276.

them will not cast them aside. Indeed, many of the great prophets of Israel—Isaiah, Jeremiah, Ezekiel, Hosea—use marriage imagery to depict the covenant between Israel and her Lord, even as they use the language of "adultery" to depict Israel's unfaithfulness. And, of course, the New Testament uses similar imagery, when the church is called the bride of Christ. Thus, our understanding of the bond of marriage is inseparably linked to and shaped by God's faithfulness to his covenant people; faith and the moral life are closely intertwined here. To men and women, then, God gives the task of learning to live together in community. Marriage is a central place, though surely not the only place, where we take up that task.

In our current cultural circumstances it is necessary to note that God's gift of marriage unites those of the opposite sex—a man and a woman. For Christians, then, there can be no such thing as same-sex marriage, though, of course, there may be deep and lasting friendships among those of the same sex. Our identity as persons is grounded in God's creation of us as bodies, and the most basic of bodily differences is that between men and women. That is why any judgment about the rightness or wrongness of same-sex genital relations ought not be isolated from our understanding of marriage more generally—as if a sexual relation cannot be wrong if it is marked by genuine care and affection. To be sure, wherever such love and affection are present, something of great human significance occurs. Nevertheless, marriage is not simply about love in general. It is about the creation of man and woman as different yet called to be true to each other. It is about the blessing of God that enables husband and wife to give birth to children and rear them. Our behavior—including our sexual activity—does not take on personal meaning and moral significance only insofar as we choose that it should.

Hence, although a friendship between two people of the same sex may be marked by deep affection, by its very nature it cannot enact the kind of moral significance that characterizes marriage. For one thing, it is, we might say, too much like the forbidden love of self. The otherness that separates spouses, an otherness that sets before them a barrier that love must constantly overcome, does not reach all the way down into the bodily difference that is fundamental to human life. And, in addition, a same-sex friendship is non-procreative. Its love-giving dimension is separate from the life-giving dimension of sexuality—and that not merely by accident, but in its very nature. The sexual relationship even of an infertile man and woman is still in accord with, not contrary to, the structure of God's creation.

In marriage, therefore, a man and a woman take up the task God sets before us in creation. They vow to live in faithful communion with one who is "other" and "different," not a mirror image of oneself. In this sense sexual ethics is never simply about sex; it is about our understanding of the human person. And a "crisis" in sexual ethics is never simply that; it is a crisis in our understanding of what it means to be a person. Are we beings characterized most of all by will and choice, beings who confer meaning and value on our acts by our choices? Or are we beings who discover meaning and value in the embodied life God has created? Because the latter is the truth, the church can offer to the world something more hopeful than the idea that what is good depends largely on our own choosing. Affirming that Jesus of Nazareth really was God in human flesh, that he now lives a bodily life in God's new creation, and that we await a day when we will share in that embodied life, the church does not offer deliverance from the body as the meaning of our hope. And, hence, part of what it means to say "Jesus is Lord" is that we commit ourselves to honoring our creation as male and female and taking up the task God sets before us in marriage. In this realm of life as in others we seek to distinguish actions that follow Christ from actions that turn in a different direction.

The created bond of marriage serves both a love-giving and a life-giving purpose in human life. The first of these, the love-giving dimension, answers to the human need for companionship. To be sure, marriage is not the only answer to that need. To suppose it is would be to miss the significance that close friendship often has in our lives. Nevertheless, involving the body as well as the emotions and the mind, the companionship of marriage offers a fuller partnership than even rich and deep friendship, and it draws us out of ourselves in a way no other human relationship does. "I am my beloved's, and his desire is for me," the bride says in the Song of Songs (7:10).

Marital love provides a context in which sexual desire can be satisfied—but satisfied in a way that treats the spouse justly. Even so, however, satisfaction of desire is not all that marriage provides. Rather, that desire is taken up into a relation marked by love, a love that seeks the good of the beloved and in so doing is itself fulfilled. Were the satisfaction of appetite all that marriage involved, we could imagine achieving that end with various partners. Love, however, aims at something more and different—a personal bond in which the beloved is not interchangeable with any other person. Hence, when desire is personalized in love, the marriage bond must be between one man and one woman, excluding all others.

Despite its great power and significance, however, even the passion of love is not all that marriage needs. The marriage vow pledges permanence, fidelity over the whole of life. But the experience of love is so powerful and so meaningful that we can easily make of it a little god and go in search of ever-new experiences of passion at the expense of permanence. This is one of the obvious ways in which we turn away from the task set before us and lose the created good of marriage. Therefore, the love that personalizes desire must itself be made steadfast and faithful by the gracious gift of God's own faithfulness. Whether or not we think of marriage as a sacrament, it is clear that the created good of marriage needs something more—namely, the grace bestowed in our baptism that empowers us for faithful living. Then, when our marriages are shaped by the love with which Christ loves his bride, the church, they can be marked by the kind of permanent fidelity Christ shows his bride.

Thus, the love-giving dimension of marriage holds together appetite, love, and fidelity. The abundant energy of sexual desire is personalized when drawn into a bond of love. And that love in turn is given permanence, made faithful by the gracious gift of God's own love.

The great gift marriage offers a husband and wife in their companionship is time—time to work out the meaning of their life together; time to take up with seriousness and joy the task of loving one who, beginning with the obvious biological difference inscribed in their bodies, is so different, so other than oneself; time for God to train them in the meaning of holiness.

This time reaches back even prior to marriage when we fall in love and begin to contemplate marriage. Often in our world couples at this point impatiently take control of the time God gives and cohabit before marriage. They tend to view this less as a step toward marriage than as a test of whether they are suited for marriage to each other. But in so doing they are training themselves to think in terms of a commitment that is shaped by the events of life rather than by a vow that reaches out creatively— with God's help—to shape the future. Likewise, the gift of time in marriage also reaches out into the future. Because the love-giving dimension of marriage involves a companionship that is so rich and so exclusive, it calls for permanence. It needs more than isolated moments of ecstasy; it needs a history in which we take up the task God sets before us in marriage, remaining faithful within the limits of the time God gives us. Thus, with respect to the time that reaches back before we marry and the time that reaches indefinitely into the future after we marry, our shared time is governed by the call to faithfulness. Indeed, we give ourselves fully only when the future is not withheld.

In the love-giving dimension of marriage a man and a woman, like Adam in the Garden, step out of their aloneness to find companionship. But this companionship is not all that marriage involves, and, indeed, left to itself it can easily become claustrophobic. We might think of children as the created cure for such possible claustrophobia, enriching the spouses' shared history. In the procreation of children, husband and wife turn outward— not individually, but together, as the one-flesh union they are. For reasons well beyond our understanding, not every marriage is blessed with children, even when they are greatly desired. But the birth of a child to husband and wife, when the gift is given, is a sign of God's continued "yes" to his creation.

In a culture such as ours, in which children are too often regarded as an entitlement, it is important to remind ourselves what it means to say that children are a gift or a blessing. When a husband and wife give themselves to each other in sexual love, they are not attempting to achieve a goal or manufacture a product. With good reason we speak of sexual ecstasy—a stepping outside oneself, outside our willed plans and projects. If, then, a child results from their mutual love, that child is a blessing bestowed on them, and they can give thanks that on this occasion their love-giving has been life-giving.

While there may be circumstances in which a couple has good reason not to have children, ordinarily Christians will welcome the blessing of children. We are not, however, obligated to have children. "Be fruitful and multiply," God's word spoken at the creation, is less a command than a blessing. Even if we read it as a command, however, we cannot forget that it has been transformed in the history of redemption. For now that The Child has been born—the child toward whom Israel's history pointed—there can be no obligation to continue the generations of humankind, although God may still bless us with the gift of children.

For reasons that do not seem to me persuasive, Roman Catholics—at least in their official teaching—have held that it is always sinful to use contraceptive methods in order to avoid having children. For a long time the reasoning behind that prohibition was that it was wrong to seek the pleasure of sexual intercourse while deliberately preventing the good (of children) to which the sexual act is naturally ordered. This rationale was destined to fail, however, and did fail once it became clear that the love-giving dimension of marriage, the companionship, was not just a pleasure but itself one of the goods of marriage. More recent Roman Catholic thought, acknowledging that there are two goods of marriage (often called unitive and procreative), has held that it is always wrong to seek one of these (the unitive) in sexual intercourse while deliberately frustrating the other (the procreative).

This, however, does not really take seriously the gift of time in marriage, the sense in which the marriage vow commits us to a lifelong, shared history. That history is more than a series of individual, isolated sexual acts; it is a union that takes shape and form over time, and that shape will necessarily differ from couple to couple. The union of husband and wife should, of course, be fruitful; that is, it should turn outward toward the world. This happens most naturally, though not exclusively or even necessarily, in the birth of children. And so long as husband and wife do not simply turn inward, focusing only on their union, contraception in itself creates no moral problem.[3] Different couples may rightly enjoy the gift of children in varying amounts and with different spacing appropriate to the particularities of their shared life. As long as a husband and a wife not only are committed

3. To be sure, however, we might need to distinguish among different kinds of contraception. Some may be more morally problematic than others.

to the good of companionship but also want their marriage to turn outward over time in order to enrich the world—so long, that is, as their union is both love-giving and life-giving—they are faithful to the Creator's gift of marriage.

When we reflect upon marriage in the light of creation, in both its love-giving and life-giving dimensions, one thing should be clear: it is not just a private matter for two individuals alone. It is, to use an older language, "the holy estate of matrimony." It exists apart from our willing and desiring. Its shape and its disciplines are not matters for us to determine, as if we were producing it *de novo*. To suppose that would be to lose the sense in which it comes to us as a gift of the Creator. To enter obediently into marriage and to accept its disciplines may seem to impinge upon our freedom, but, in fact, it is a gift that connects our lives and our generations over time, making glad our hearts.

The Marriage Bond in Need of Healing

The good gift of marriage written into the structure of creation is, of course, like the rest of life, damaged and disordered by our sin. Hence, we cannot simply assume that the desires and inclinations that seem to come naturally to us coincide with the will of the Creator. It is surely no accident that, as the monastic movement gradually took shape in the church, one of the human impulses that the monks sought to discipline through a commitment to chastity was sexual desire. They had a sense of the fragility of human life, of the way in which anarchic desire can in a few moments of passion destroy the shared life people have worked hard to build.

Therefore, as a gift of the God who seeks to make us whole, marriage takes on a healing dimension in addition to its love-giving and life-giving dimensions. For even when appetite and desire are personalized in love—when, that is, they are directed toward just one person who is not interchangeable with any other—love remains fickle and all too transitory. By itself it may not be sufficient to sustain a lifelong commitment. Hence, as Kierkegaard noted, the marriage vow "contains the apparent contradiction" that love becomes a duty.[4] Contrary to our normal way of thinking, it is duty that gives freedom, the freedom that comes not from following our impulses but from living with an abandonment that is disciplined and shaped in such a way that it is protected against the instability of appetite and love.

Thus God begins to heal the wound that egocentric sin inflicts on our sexual nature. Just as the prohibition of fornication frees us to have, without fear, friendships with those of the opposite sex, just as the prohibition of homosexual behavior frees us to have, without fear, friendships with those of the same sex, even so the prohibition of adultery frees us to give ourselves permanently and exclusively to a spouse.[5] Thus does God begin to keep the promise hidden in the commandment, the promise that he will heal our wayward desires and fickle loves and begin to make of us people who are faithful in love.

In marriage, therefore, God sets before us a task. A husband gradually becomes a person who can love his wife faithfully over time, and she likewise learns what it means to live out her commitment to him. Whatever the twists and turns of life, whatever other possible sexual partners may come along, God is at work in the institution of marriage to shape and form us into the people he promises we will be—people who shall not commit adultery because their hearts have been made steadfast in love. And this,

4. Søren Kierkegaard, *Works of Love* (New York: Harper Torchbooks, 1962), 40.
5. Although I can no longer trace its history, I am quite certain that I owe this way of formulating the healing dimension of marriage to a communication many years ago from Paul Rainbow, professor of New Testament at Sioux Falls Seminary.

we might note, is why for Christians there can be no such thing as a trial marriage, no such thing as cohabitation aimed at determining whether we are really suited for marriage. For, on the contrary, the task God sets before us is not that of trying to determine whether we are prepared to promise faithfulness to this other person. The task, rather, is to hand over our future in the marriage vow, undertaking life together as a task set before us, part of the curriculum in the school of God's commandments.

Once we take this healing dimension of marriage seriously, we have to ask ourselves about the possibility of divorce. Should it or can it have any place at all within a Christian understanding of marriage? Is not divorce essentially a turning away from the promise that God will use marriage to heal our wayward impulses?

We need only consider the three dimensions of marriage to appreciate why divorce is such a serious matter. The love-giving dimension, with its focus on the promise of faithful companionship, reminds us that this promise answers to a deep human need: the longing never to be left entirely alone, whatever the future may bring. And marriage gives rise to a set of expectations in one's spouse that ought not be disappointed.

The life-giving dimension of marriage focuses on the children who may be born to husband and wife. Parents are not just a cause and children an effect that we can easily separate. Children embody in their flesh a marital union, a union that spouses intending to divorce propose to rupture. We should not be surprised if this disturbs a child—even a grown child—at the very center of his or her identity. Clearly, this life-giving dimension reminds us that marriage is not simply a matter of private agreement between husband and wife to marry or to dissolve their marriage.

Finally, marriage can hardly function as a place of healing if we refuse its disciplines. In marriage God proposes to school us in the meaning of love for and commitment to another. There are no guarantees that the tasks set before us in the curriculum of this school will always be easy or pleasant. But marriage cannot be a place of healing if we abandon it whenever our desires and wishes move us to do so. Rather, in marriage we are given an opportunity to try to be as faithful to one person as God has been to us in Jesus. We should note how the Israelite prophets offer renewal of the covenant even after Israel has gone after other gods. Thus, for example, through Jeremiah (3:12) God speaks to the northern kingdom of Israel: "Return, faithless Israel. . . . I will not look on you in anger, for I am merciful." So also, our call to marital fidelity is embedded in the biblical depiction of the LORD's covenant with Israel. This means that, as Patrick Miller notes, "the assumption that punishment and dissolution of the marriage relationship are the only options is undercut in the way in which the mercy of God leads to renewal of the covenant."[6]

Obviously, therefore, we may not take the possibility of divorce lightly. What we say more specifically about it must be determined by how we understand the rather ambiguous New Testament teaching on the permanence of marriage. Jesus' words in Luke 16:18, though fitting uncertainly into their context, would seem to be clear: "Every one who divorces his wife and marries another commits adultery, and he who marries a woman divorced from her husband commits adultery."[7] But the saying as recorded in Matthew 19:9 includes permission (though certainly not a requirement) for divorce if one's spouse has been unfaithful: "Whoever divorces his wife, except for unchastity, and marries another, commits adultery." Thus, whereas the saying in Luke 16 (and Mark 10:11–12), read apart from Matthew 19, seems to say

6. Miller, *Ten Commandments*, 289.
7. Essentially the same teaching, with the addition of an exception for "unchastity," appears in the Sermon on the Mount (Matt. 5:31–32). Jesus' saying in Mark 10:11–12 also repeats this teaching and adds that the same would be true if a wife were to divorce her husband.

that whoever divorces and then marries another has committed adultery, the exception clause added in Matthew complicates the issue. It seems to say that whoever divorces and then marries another has committed adultery, except in the case where the spouse had been unfaithful. Thus, in Matthew 19 remarriage is not characterized as adulterous if the divorce has been because of unfaithfulness. Only if the divorce itself was wrong is the remarriage also wrong.

Still more nuances are present in St. Paul's discussion of marriage in 1 Corinthians 7. The Corinthians had, it seems, written Paul to seek his counsel about several matters pertaining to marriage, among them divorce. He first underscores what is not simply his advice but is the teaching of Jesus as it had come to him ("I give charge, not I but the Lord"). This teaching is that "the wife should not separate from her husband (but if she does, let her remain single or else be reconciled to her husband)—and that the husband should not divorce his wife" (1 Cor. 7:10–11). Here there is no permission for the spouse who has initiated the divorce to remarry. What about the spouse who did not? About that the passage is simply silent, neither expressly forbidding nor permitting remarriage.

In the following verses, however, Paul goes beyond the teaching of Jesus known to him and adds his own advice ("I say, not the Lord") about questions that could have arisen only within the context of the church's mission to the Gentiles. What if a Christian man or woman was married to someone who was not a Christian? Paul's first move is to urge that the Christian husband or wife should not pursue a divorce simply because the spouse does not name Jesus as Lord. But if the spouse who is not a Christian desires a divorce and they cannot be reconciled, the believing "brother or sister is not bound" (1 Cor. 7:15). Here then is one place—when an unbelieving spouse chooses to divorce—that Paul clearly permits remarriage.

Where does this collection of passages leave us? The first thing to say is that these passages surely view divorce with far more seriousness than many Christians do today. The church's way of life has not been strong enough to resist tendencies within the broader culture. Our first word to those in troubled marriages should not be one that contemplates the possibility or permissibility of divorce. If our churches regularly offer remarriage to divorced Christians, paying little attention to the New Testament witness, we forfeit the right to be taken seriously when we try to teach about sexuality and marriage.

At least in principle, Roman Catholicism has tried to do better, though not without considerable strain in recent years. Thus, the *Catechism of the Catholic Church*, quoting canon law, teaches that "a ratified and consummated marriage" between baptized Christians "cannot be dissolved by any human power or for any reason other than death." In such cases, then, a husband or wife who seeks a divorce from the civil authorities attempts what is actually impossible. And if he or she remarries, "the remarried spouse is then in a situation of public and permanent adultery."[8]

Still, one cannot, as I noted, adhere to this position without considerable strain. Baptized Christians who have divorced and remarried (in civil law) and who therefore live "in a situation of public and permanent adultery" cannot, the *Catechism* teaches, "receive Eucharistic communion as long as this situation persists."[9] And that is true even of a spouse who was "the innocent victim of a divorce decreed by civil law" and who therefore "has not contravened the moral law." "There is," the *Catechism* continues, "a considerable difference between a spouse who has sincerely tried to be faithful to the sacrament of marriage and is unjustly abandoned, and one who through his own grave

8. *Catechism of the Catholic Church* (Mahwah, NJ: Paulist Press, 1994), paragraphs 2382 and 2384.
9. *Catechism of the Catholic Church*, par. 1650.

fault destroys a canonically valid marriage."[10] Just not enough difference, evidently, to permit eucharistic communion. This is not easy to understand in the case of persons who neither desired nor initiated their divorce, are now (civilly) remarried, and hence—even though assured that they should "not consider themselves separated from the Church"[11]—may not participate in the church's Eucharist.

That many Christians in our culture end their marriages—and then remarry—for reasons that have no New Testament warrant is surely obvious; neither our teaching nor our practice should suggest that we approve what they do. But the question is whether we can also acknowledge that sometimes marriages are genuinely destroyed by infidelity and other times may just burn themselves out and come to an end—and whether we can acknowledge that in at least some of these cases the opportunity to remarry may mean that God is calling us anew to a task from which we once turned away. We should not underestimate the power of God's faithfulness to renew our own.

Even in cases where the believer wanting to undertake a second marriage has sincerely tried to be faithful in his or her first marriage and has been unjustly abandoned, the church must be certain that its acceptance of this second marriage does not seem to undermine its public teaching about marriage and divorce. What this requires is a (re)marriage ceremony that does not simply act as if nothing significant or sinful had happened when one (or perhaps both) of those who now comes for marriage was previously divorced. In such circumstances the marriage rite should publicly acknowledge that a broken marriage vow is evidence of our failure, evidence that calls for confession of that failure and prayer for forgiveness. Only if something like that becomes

10. *Catechism of the Catholic Church*, par. 2386.
11. *Catechism of the Catholic Church*, par. 1651.

our practice is there any chance of restoring genuine integrity to what we say and do with respect to marriage, while also not treating those who have been "unjustly abandoned" as if they were, in fact, separated from the church.

The Marriage Bond and the Promised Redemption

When in the last book of the New Testament, the Revelation to St. John, the promised new heaven and earth are envisioned, the image of the New Jerusalem is not that of a political kingdom, a family, or a church—but rather, of a marriage. "I saw the holy city, new Jerusalem, coming down out of heaven from God, prepared as a bride adorned for her husband" (Rev. 21:2).[12] And the seer is instructed to write, "Blessed are those who are invited to the marriage supper of the Lamb" (19:9). That supper is the great end-time marriage feast of Christ and his bride, the church. Karl Barth notes the "striking fact" that the Greek word for marriage (*gamos*) is used only once in the New Testament (Heb. 13:4) to refer specifically to marriage. It denotes more precisely the wedding banquet and refers "almost always to the eschatological marriage feast of Christ the Bridegroom."[13]

This should remind us of the deepest truth about the marriage vow we take. It is a promise of faithful companionship until death parts us. Marriage is an earthly reality, given us by God so that we may be happy in the companionship it provides. Nonetheless, marriage exists not just to make us happy but to make us holy. It is one of the created schools of virtue through which God makes of us faithful people. What our earthly marriages will be like when they have been buried with Christ and

---

12. Note also Rev. 21:22: "I saw no temple in the city."

13. Karl Barth, *Church Dogmatics* III/4, ed. G. W. Bromiley and T. F. Torrance, trans. A. T. Mackay et al. (Edinburgh: T&T Clark, 1961), 143–44.

raised to new life in the Lamb's marriage supper we cannot really imagine. All that has been made holy will in some way—however transformed and perfected—remain, but we should not suppose that a heavenly reunion which simply resumes earthly marriage is the goal God has in mind for us.

> We were made for God. Only by being in some respect like Him, only by being a manifestation of His beauty, lovingkindness, wisdom or goodness, has any earthly Beloved excited our love. It is not that we have loved them too much, but that we did not quite understand what we were loving. It is not that we shall be asked to turn from them, so dearly familiar, to a Stranger. When we see the face of God we shall know that we have always known it. . . . In Heaven there will be no anguish and no duty of turning away from our earthly Beloveds. . . . We shall find them all in Him. By loving Him more than them we shall love them more than we now do.[14]

Once we understand this, we can also appreciate how those who are not married play an important role in the church's life and witness. Within Christian history there have, of course, been some—especially in monastic communities—who have understood themselves as called by God to a celibate life. This is, as Robert Jenson nicely puts it, "not a renunciation of sexuality but a pressurized form of it, a reduction of eroticism to that eros between God and his people that is the enabling archetype of all eroticism."[15] For many believers, however, the single life has less the character of a commitment than an accident of one's personal history. But they too are called to table at the marriage supper

14. C. S. Lewis, *The Four Loves* (New York: Harcourt Brace Jovanovich, 1960), 190–91.
15. Robert W. Jenson, "Male and Female He Created Them," in *I Am the Lord Your God: Christian Reflections on the Ten Commandments*, ed. Carl E. Braaten and Christopher R. Seitz (Grand Rapids: Eerdmans, 2005), 186.

of the Lamb. Therefore, they remind us all that restoration of our earthly marriages is not the point of the new creation God has in mind. The church badly needs those who are not married to protect us against the recurring temptation to make marriage more ultimate than it is and to miss the sense in which all our earthly loves—marital love included—must be transformed and reborn when we take our place at the wedding feast of Christ and his bride.

This is how we are to think of marriage in the light of redemption. "You shall not commit adultery." We should listen for the promise in that command. You *shall* love the Lord God with all your heart, soul, and mind. You *shall* be a bride eager to greet her bridegroom.

❧ CHAPTER 3 ❧

The Family Bond

Honor your father and your mother, that your days may be long
in the land which the LORD your God gives you.

Exodus 20:12

The community that binds husband and wife in marriage is,
of course, closely (though not inevitably) allied with the bond
between parents and children—and then with the larger unfolding of kinship relations over generations. As with the marriage
bond, the community of the family is also a school of virtue,
given in part to develop in us the capacity to love.

The commandment itself refers specifically to the bond between parents and their children: "Honor your father and your
mother." There is, however, a long tradition in Christian interpretation of expanding the commandment's reach. So, for example,
Calvin takes it to mean that we should look up not just to parents
but also "to those whom God has placed over us, and should treat
them with honor, obedience, and gratefulness."[1] Likewise, and

---

1. John Calvin, *Institutes of the Christian Religion*, ed. John T. McNeill, trans.
Ford Lewis Battles, Library of Christian Classics 20 (Philadelphia: Westminster,
1960), 2.8.35.

much more recently, the *Catechism of the Catholic Church* understands the requirement of honor and respect to apply to "all those whom God, for our good, has vested with his authority."[2]

In the past, Christian thinkers sometimes tended to conflate paternal authority with kingly authority—picturing fathers as monarchs on a small scale, and all other authority as derived from that of parents. And Christians should no doubt give proper respect and, when appropriate, obedience to teachers, employers, and government officials. Nevertheless, it may be better to treat the fourth commandment more narrowly, confining it to the bond between parents and their children. For political community and familial community are not two instances of the same kind of bond. St. Augustine was right, in the famous discussion in book 19 of *The City of God*, to demythologize the sphere of politics, to see it as limited and as formed more by shared interests than by mutual love. Indeed, when the kings of the earth bring their glory to the New Jerusalem (Rev. 21:24) and the wolf and lamb feed together (Isa. 65:25), political rule will be no more.

Whatever we may say about other forms of association—such as the political—in which one person exercises authority over another, the bond that unites parents and children in familial community is unique. When we honor our parents, we do here on earth what Jesus, the Son of the Father, does in eternity.[3] And when parents love their children and teach them to live in truth before God, they do what the heavenly Father does.[4] Hence, although parents discipline their children and strive to shape their character, they do more than this. They bear witness to

2. *Catechism of the Catholic Church* (Mahwah, NJ: Paulist Press, 1994), par. 2197.

3. "Truly, truly, I say to you, the Son can do nothing of his own accord, but only what he sees the Father doing; for whatever he does, that the Son does likewise" (John 5:19).

4. "For the Father loves the Son, and shows him all that he himself is doing" (John 5:20).

their children that together they stand under God's authority and that God alone can secure their lives. That work of loving witness never ends, not even when parental discipline ceases.

The Family Bond in Creation

Although it seems clear that the commandments of the Decalogue were addressed primarily to adults, I suspect that our use of the fourth commandment has probably focused more often than not on the relation between younger children and their parents. No doubt that is because this is the context in which we can understand the required honor to imply obedience, and in that way pour some reasonably specific meaning into the commandment; for it is probably easier to say what it means to obey than to honor. Nor is it wrong to emphasize obedience. After all, the Letter to the Ephesians (6:1–3) clearly seems to take the requirement of honor for parents to mean, at the least, obedience.

Even if we start with the need for children to obey their parents, the commandment will hardly be unambiguous. For one thing, the larger biblical context itself makes clear how complicated this can be. Rebekah is a deceptive and scheming mother; Lot is hardly a model father; Jonathan's relation to his father, Saul, is marked as much by duplicity as by obedience; Absalom's disobedience casts light not only on his character but also on the failures of David as his father. And, of course, as Jesus makes clear—a point to which we will return—the family bond presupposed by the fourth commandment is always radically qualified by the first.[5] Moreover, when the commandment to honor and obey one's parents is directly taken up in the New Testament

5. "He who loves father or mother more than me is not worthy of me; and he who loves son or daughter more than me is not worthy of me" (Matt. 10:37).

(in Eph. 6 and Col. 3), the requirement is not only that children should obey their parents but also that fathers should treat their children well, not provoking them to anger. So obligation and responsibility run in both directions.

Clearly, the commandment's instruction goes well beyond the obvious fact that any command to obey another human being must have its limits. Nor is obedience at the core of the honor that is commanded. More fundamental is the need for gratitude, which clearly has no age limit. Thus Calvin says that the required honoring of parents includes reverence, obedience, and gratitude.[6] Likewise Luther, in his Large Catechism, having mentioned honor and obedience, adds that "it is our duty before the world to show gratitude for the kindness and for all the good things we have received from our parents."[7] And the *Catechism of the Catholic Church* teaches: "Respect for parents (*filial piety*) derives from *gratitude* toward those who, by the gift of life, their love and their work, have brought their children into the world and enabled them to grow in stature, wisdom, and grace."[8]

In the requirement of gratitude we encounter the commandment's deepest puzzle. After all, there is a certain contingency in the parent-child bond. "What's in a name?" Juliet asks Romeo. The fact that she is a Capulet and he is from the rival Montague clan should, she thinks, be no barrier to their love. "O, be some other name!" she says. Her point is simple and straightforward: nothing except biology, nothing except the purely accidental fact of their birth into opposed families, separates them—and it therefore amounts to, precisely, nothing. And if it is purely accidental that this man and this woman are my parents, if rather

6. Calvin, *Institutes* 2.8.36.
7. Robert Kolb and Timothy J. Wengert, eds., *The Book of Concord: The Confessions of the Evangelical Lutheran Church* (Minneapolis: Fortress, 2000), 404.
8. *Catechism of the Catholic Church*, par. 2215.

than choosing this bond I simply found myself in it, why am I obligated to show them gratitude? Understandably, the sheer givenness of the relation can sometimes be experienced as a burden.

Nevertheless, being burdened by our children, parents, and siblings is part of what it means to belong to a family. Families would not be nearly as important to us as they are if the simple fact of the familial bond did not give us claims on each other. The point of the givenness of the biological bond, the significance we see in it, is that our families are not formed by contracts. Rather, we find that we have been given to each other, and we are challenged to find moral meaning in that simple fact and in the unchosen burdens it places upon us. Here we learn to deal with what is unwanted and unexpected in life. We are drawn out of our natural self-concern and burdened both for the sake of others and also for our own good.

Hence, the commandment exists to remind us that the family bond, even if sometimes burdensome, is a gift—and a gift that calls for our gratitude. The puzzling givenness of the parent-child bond is simply a focused instance of the puzzling givenness of all existence—the mystery that anything should exist at all. Allowing ourselves to be instructed by the commandment, we can learn to see moral meaning embedded in the biological relation. Children are "a heritage from the LORD" (Ps. 127:3), a sign of God's continuing "yes" to his creation and to the human beings with whom he wills to live in covenant community. To be sure, we are also more than our biology and are free to some extent to transcend our embeddedness in the natural world. Part of that freedom, however, consists in our ability to discern significance in the contingencies of life, to be grateful for the parents who gave us life and nurtured us.

The child's gratitude answers to the parents' life-giving generosity. The desire to have children expresses a deeply humanistic impulse to be faithful to the heavenly Father's own self-spending creative power, in which we are allowed to participate. That will-ingness to give birth, to trust in God's continuing "yes" to the creation, expresses, as Gabriel Marcel so nicely puts it, "a fun-damental generosity."[9] If children really are a heritage from the LORD, they are neither products of our will nor objects that we design. They are, as Christians have always understood, not an entitlement to which we have a right, but a gift and a blessing. A man and a woman give themselves to each other in love, and, in the mystery of God's providence, that love-giving is sometimes life-giving. Part of the blessing is that we are free to accept our children as they come to us, free from any need to exercise the kind of "quality control" we do over objects that we make.

Understanding the parent-child bond in this way, we should also understand what is troubling about the increasing use of as-sisted reproduction techniques. Christians confess in the creeds that Jesus, the Son of God the Father, is *begotten* of the Father from eternity—"begotten, not made," as the Nicene Creed puts it. Why? To make clear that Jesus is truly God, that he shares equally with his Father (and their Spirit) in the divine life. Were he made—that is, were he a creature, even first among creatures—he would not share equally in the being of his Maker. Analogously, to know our children as begotten, not made, is a way of affirm-ing that they share equally with us in the dignity of human life.

To the degree that we begin to think of our children as prod-ucts made by human ingenuity, we may find it increasingly hard simply to welcome them as our equals, as a gift bestowed upon the loving embrace of a man and a woman. It will become easier to think of them as existing to satisfy our desire for a child (and, perhaps, a child of a certain sort) than as the manifestation of God's continued commitment to the creation. It will be easier to

9. Gabriel Marcel, "The Mystery of the Family," in *Homo Viator: Introduction to the Metaphysic of Hope* (New York: Harper Torchbooks, 1962), 91.

think of parenthood as "making," as a project we undertake, as a right of which we should not be deprived, than as the exercise of fundamental generosity that Marcel discerns in the mystery of procreation.

This does not mean that parents do not and should not shape the character of their children in important ways. On the contrary, they stand before their children as God's representatives precisely in order to tell a story, to initiate their children into a way of life. Thus, a central theme in the biblical account of the institution of the Passover is that when children ask what the meaning of these rituals is, their father is to tell them the story of deliverance from Egypt.[10] The same is true with respect to the commandments given to shape Israel's life. It is worth quoting in full the charge given to parents in Deuteronomy 6:20–25.

> When your son asks you in time to come, "What is the meaning of the testimonies and the statutes and the ordinances which the LORD our God has commanded you?" then you shall say to your son, "We were Pharaoh's slaves in Egypt; and the LORD brought us out of Egypt with a mighty hand; and the LORD showed signs and wonders, great and grievous, against Egypt and against Pharaoh and all his household, before our eyes; and he brought us out from there, that he might bring us in and give us the land which he swore to give to our fathers. And the LORD commanded us to do all these statutes, to fear the LORD our God, for our good always, that he might preserve us alive, as at this day. And it will be righteousness for us, if we are careful to do all this commandment before the LORD our God, as he has commanded us."

The New Testament makes the same point very directly, even if less poetically: parents should rear their children "in the discipline and instruction of the Lord" (Eph. 6:4).

10. Cf. Exod. 12:26–27.

Clearly, therefore, the created meaning of the family bond points not only to begetting but also to nurture. Parents initiate their children into the human inheritance, at the center of which is the story of God's covenant faithfulness to humankind. This is, of course, a venture that can only be done in the hope that God will be what we cannot be, the guarantor of the future of our children.

The Family Bond in Need of Healing

The presence of families in which parents commit themselves to the nurture of their children, and children, in turn, honor and obey their parents will not save a world disordered by sin. But such families—in which parents gladly sacrifice on behalf of their children, and the sacrifices are received by their children with gratitude—may achieve a lesser but significant good. They enable our societies to live in relative peace and cooperation, and perhaps even to flourish within the limits of human history. Just as important, as the basic unit of society the family witnesses to the limits of political power, and family loyalty offers a kind of protection against the tendency toward tyranny of those who rule.[11]

At the same time we have to acknowledge that the family, essential as it is to human well-being, presents us with problems we must live with but can never completely "solve" in this life. We will see this if we try to take seriously the claim made in the *Catechism of the Catholic Church* that "in every human person [we see] a son or daughter of the One who wants to be called 'our Father.'"[12] This might seem to suggest that we must learn to expand our loves beyond the limits that come naturally to

11. This, we might note, is another reason why it is unwise to conflate paternal with political authority in our interpretations of the fourth commandment.
12. *Catechism of the Catholic Church*, par. 2212.

us. Jesus, after all, asks, "If you salute only your brethren, what
more are you doing than others?" (Matt. 5:47). But one of the
limits that comes so naturally to us is the family, and, as Michael
Walzer has succinctly put it, "favoritism begins in the family."[13]

Hence, if we want (and need) the goods of social harmony, cooperation, sacrifice for future generations, and protection against
an all-encompassing political sphere that healthy families make
possible, we must, it seems, accept inequalities that are built into
the nature of familial love. We must reckon with the ambiguities
of family loyalty. Parents, after all, are not just public function-
aries charged with caring for a few young citizens of the polity.
They have special attachment to their children, preferential love
for those children, and a willingness to devote a considerable portion of their resources to their children's well-being. Moreover,
knowing that they are loved in this way—with a "guarantee of
love"—is in large part what helps children grow into adults who
are themselves capable of commitment to others.[14]

It seems, therefore, that in this life we must learn to live as
best we can within the tension between love for those nearest to
us, those to whom we owe special care and gratitude, and love
for those more distant from us who, even in their distance, are
(like us) sons or daughters of the One who wants to be called
our Father. To fail in obligations that the family bond entails
is to give way to sin; yet, to permit the special claims of those
for whom a certain preference is appropriate to blind us to the
need to expand our loves beyond what comes naturally is also to
give way to sin. No cookbook can give us a recipe for resolving
perfectly these competing claims upon us; they must simply be
lived and, even, suffered in a world in which the needs of near
and distant neighbors are not easily harmonized and in which
our own desires and inclinations are all too often disordered.

13. Michael Walzer, *Spheres of Justice* (New York: Basic Books, 1983), 229.
14. Walzer, *Spheres of Justice*, 239.

Of the various ways in which our disordered desires that need healing disrupt the bond between parents and children, we cannot ignore the continuing evil of abortion; for it goes to the very heart of the familial bond. It testifies to our inability to see the conception and birth of a child as a sign of God's continued "yes" to the creation. It enacts a refusal—not just on the part of mothers, but at least as often by fathers—to understand the family as a place in which we are rightly burdened by each other. In permitting some of us to exercise unlimited power over the lives of others of us, it undermines our commitment to equal human dignity.

Surely Christians more than others should not fail to see that even the youngest and weakest among us—even the fetus hidden in the darkness of the womb—is, in all stages of life, equally one of us. As G. K. Chesterton once noted, Christian literature and art down through the centuries have "rung the changes on that single paradox; that the hands that had made the sun and stars were too small to reach the huge heads of the cattle."[15] Theologians and Christian leaders often bemoan the divisions that undermine the church's witness in the world, but if we are serious about that, we should repent of the church's failure to give an undivided witness against the acceptance and, even, affirmation of abortion in our world.

This does not mean that there are no hard cases in which abortion might be permitted (though surely not morally required)— cases in which the mother's life cannot be saved without an intervention that also causes the fetus to die or cases in which the woman's pregnancy results from forcible intercourse.[16] But for

15. G. K. Chesterton, *The Everlasting Man* (New York: Image Books, 1955), 168.
16. For a discussion of such hard cases and of the general problems with arguments supporting abortion, see the following: Gilbert Meilaender, *Bioethics: A Primer for Christians*, 3rd ed. (Grand Rapids: Eerdmans, 2013), chap. 3; and Meilaender, *Body, Soul, and Bioethics* (Notre Dame and London: University of Notre Dame Press, 1995), chap. 5.

us to make those relatively few cases the center of discussion is, I
fear, less a way of grappling with the problem than a flight from
encountering it. As long as we focus our attention on a few possible exceptions to the general prohibition of abortion, we position ourselves in a sheltered place where reflection and discussion
are unlikely ever to come to an end. Immersing ourselves, as is
probable, in talk of doing the deed regretfully and mournfully, we
all too easily end in a position once characterized by Paul Ramsey
as "ample abortions always with tears."[17] We do not solve the
problem of unwanted children by sweeping the doorstep free of
them every day in order to remove them from our sight.

What, then, are we to do about the countless number of orphaned children in the world? In many cases, after all, they need
a place of familial belonging not because their parents would
not care for them but because their parents could not do so. In
a disordered world badly in need of reconciliation, Christians
must surely be people who bring the good news of adoption.
Having received what St. Paul calls "adoption as sons," we are
enabled by the Spirit to call God "Father."[18] We know, therefore,
that the family bond is not simply a matter of biology. The
adoption that is at the heart of the New Testament gospel has
its analogue in the life of our societies when children who lack
a place of familial belonging are adopted and enabled now to
call a man and woman "father" and "mother."

There is loss here, of course. The adopted child will, at least
to some degree, have lost the connection with his or her biological parents established in creation. The birth parents, and
probably most especially the birth mother, may suffer from the
loss of that bond, even if they felt unable to sustain it. And the
adoptive parents, if it happens that they are infertile, may regret

17. Paul Ramsey, "Abortion: A Review Article," *The Thomist* 37 (January 1973):
205.
18. Gal. 4:4–7.

their inability to procreate. Acknowledging such loss, we should nevertheless recall words spoken by Pope John Paul II to a meeting of adoptive families: "To adopt a child is a great *work of love*. When it is done, much is given, but much is also received. It is a true exchange of gifts."[19] When adoptive parents understand that they are standing in for birth parents, and when a child in need of parental nurture receives it, the disorder of our world is at least partially healed. Indeed, adoption may help us all to learn that children are never our possession and that all parents, whether biological or adoptive, receive their children as gifts and are called to accept their parenthood as a lifelong commitment. We may hope that such generosity on their part is met with gratitude on the part of their children.

The Family Bond and the Promised Redemption

Although the bond between parents and children is deeply embedded within the structure of creation, its limits are set by the first commandment. Whoever "loves father or mother more than me is not worthy of me," Jesus says, "and he who loves son or daughter more than me is not worthy of me" (Matt. 10:37). In Luke's story of the boy Jesus in the temple (2:41–52), the claims of the "Father's house" set limits to the parental claims of Joseph and Mary, and in the very different story of the wedding at Cana, the Gospel of John makes clear (2:4) that the demands of Jesus' calling set limits to Mary's claim upon him.

In the death and resurrection of Jesus the creation experiences (in advance) its end and moves toward the promised new

19. John Paul II, "Address of the Holy Father John Paul II to the Meeting of the Adoptive Families Organized by the Missionaries of Charity," September 5, 2000, http://w2.vatican.va/content/john-paul-ii/en/speeches/2000/jul-sep/docu ments/hf_jp-ii_spe_20000905_adozioni.html.

creation. Disturbing as it may seem to us, therefore, Karl Barth rightly says that "there is an orphaned state required for the sake of the kingdom of heaven."[20] For some (few, we may hope) the call to follow Jesus can mean that "a man's foes will be those of his own household" (Matt. 10:36). Of course, no one should be eager or quick to assume that Jesus has called him to this orphaned state. C. S. Lewis made that point nicely: "The hard sayings of our Lord are wholesome to those only who find them hard. There is a terrible chapter in M. Mauriac's *Vie de Jesus*. When the Lord spoke of brother and child against parent, the other disciples were horrified. Not so Judas. He took to it as a duck takes to water."[21] But if the call to such radical discipleship, when it comes, is experienced as deeply painful, then we may be confident that it comes "as a message from the *eschaton.*"[22]

Apart from such extraordinary and painful circumstances, how shall we understand the family bond in relation to God's redemptive purposes? It serves, by God's grace, as a school of virtue in which we begin to be formed as people who will love and honor our heavenly Father. The honor and obedience we give to our parents should, as Calvin writes, be "a step toward honoring that highest Father."[23] More fundamentally still, we may become people marked by gratitude for the gift of life and the beauties of creation. These gifts come, as Luther puts it in the Small Catechism's explanation of the first article of the Creed, from the Creator's "fatherly and divine goodness and mercy." And therefore, as we learn within the family what it means to be grateful, we may learn a still more basic gratitude: "to thank

20. Karl Barth, *Church Dogmatics* III/4, ed. G. W. Bromiley and T. F. Torrance, trans. A. T. Mackay et al. (Edinburgh: T&T Clark, 1961), 261.
21. C. S. Lewis, *God in the Dock* (Grand Rapids: Eerdmans, 1970), 191–92.
22. Barth, *Church Dogmatics* III/4, 265.
23. Calvin, *Institutes* 2.8.38.

and praise, serve and obey" the One by whom and for whom
we are made.[24] With hearts marked by gratitude learned in that
school of virtue, we can become people who are eager to live in
the new creation God promises.

To understand the family bond as a school of virtue in which
we may learn to desire life with God and with all who will share
in the redeemed creation testifies to its importance, and we
should probably not try to say more than this. So, for example,
we should draw back from the relatively recent Roman Catholic tendency to speak of the Christian family as a "domestic
church."[25] To be sure, the family is not simply a clan delimited
by biological ties; for, as we have seen, the familial tie can be
formed not just through biology but also through adoption. But
at the same time, the family is also not yet the church in which
all who follow Jesus are, simply, brothers and sisters. We cannot
see clearly or say with certainty how our family bonds will be
taken up into the promised new creation, but we know that they
will be transformed—a transformation to which the church must
witness here and now. An important part of the church's witness
is given in the lives of those who are unmarried or childless. It is
their vocation to remind us that the church grows not because
of our natural capacity to give birth but through the grace of
our adoption as God's children.

The story told in the Old Testament begins with a family
torn by a conflict, seen most strikingly in Cain's murder of his
brother Abel. And the more specific story of Israel is the story
of the family of Abraham and Sarah, which is also marked by
deception, conflict, and rivalry. But the Old Testament ends with
the assurance of Malachi (4:5–6) that when "the great and terrible day of the LORD comes," it will be a day of redemption

---

24. Kolb and Wengert, *Book of Concord*, 354–55.
25. See, e.g., *Catechism of the Catholic Church*, par. 2204.

and healing—a day when the hearts of fathers will be turned to their children and the hearts of children to their fathers. In that day we will see the promise buried in the command. As Jesus has done from eternity, so we too shall be children who love the Father, and we will live long in the land God gives us.

CHAPTER 4

The Life Bond

You shall not kill.

Exodus 20:13

The life bond, uniting all human beings as it does, is likely to seem less intense and more abstract than the special relationship we share with a spouse or a family member. And, in fact, it *should* seem more abstract. If I seem to love humanity in general more than those in my family whom I see every day, we have good reason to doubt whether my love for humanity amounts to much. It is more likely to be the sort of "telescopic philanthropy" that Charles Dickens satirically depicts in *Bleak House* in the character of Mrs. Jellyby, who high-mindedly devotes herself to African missions while caring very little for the needs of her family. Even the claim to love God is empty, we are taught in 1 John (4:20), if we do not love the brother or sister whom we see daily. With good reason, therefore, one of the best prayer books ever written invites us to pray: "Forbid that I should refuse to my own household the courtesy and politeness which I think proper to show to strangers. Let charity to-day begin at home."[1] What begins at home should not end there, however—a truth that is underscored by the fifth commandment.

The Life Bond in Creation

"The purpose of this commandment," Calvin writes, is that "the Lord has bound mankind together by a certain unity; hence each man ought to concern himself with the safety of all."[2] Calvin offers two reasons for affirming a life bond that unites all human beings. First, all have been made in the image of God, and hence, each must see others as his equals. And second, even apart from the God-relation, we share a common bond of humanity. "If you prick us," asks Shylock, "do we not bleed?"[3]

The covenant that God makes with Noah and his descendants after the great flood focuses first of all on the bond that unites all *human* lives. "Whoever sheds the blood of man, by man shall his blood be shed; for God made man in his own image" (Gen. 9:6). That humankind has a special relation to the Creator becomes even clearer when we remind ourselves who this Creator is. He is the One who in Jesus, the incarnate Son of the Father, has taken human life into his own divine life. When we see the face of Christ in every human face, we realize that the commandment to respect the life of every human being has its ground not only in our common humanity but also and preeminently in the fact that the Creator stands beside us and shares our life with us.

1. John Baillie, *A Diary of Private Prayer* (New York: Scribner's Sons, 1949), 89.
2. John Calvin, *Institutes of the Christian Religion*, ed. John T. McNeill, trans. Ford Lewis Battles, Library of Christian Classics 20 (Philadelphia: Westminster, 1960), 2.8.39.
3. William Shakespeare, *The Merchant of Venice*, III.i.61.

By contrast, that same covenant with Noah expressly permits human beings to make use of the other animals as food. This does not mean, however, that animals are beyond the scope of God's concern. When the LORD says that he will establish his covenant with Noah and his descendants, he adds, in the same breath, "and with every living creature that is with you, the birds, the cattle, and every beast of the earth with you" (Gen. 9:10). Plants and animals may be used to sustain human life, but they do not exist solely for that purpose. God causes grass to grow for the cattle, and he makes high mountains for the goats, and rocks as a refuge for badgers.[4] "Even the sparrow finds a home," the psalmist (84:3) says—and why not, since, as Jesus himself says (Matt. 10:29), the heavenly Father knows when even one such sparrow falls to the ground.

Nevertheless, to some the Decalogue might seem to need a supplement, an additional commandment specifically requiring our care for the nonhuman creation, our love not only for God and the neighbor but also for the earth. Thus, in 1939 Walter Lowdermilk, a soil conservationist, gave a speech calling for an "eleventh commandment": "Thou shalt inherit the holy earth as a faithful steward conserving its resources and productivity from generation to generation. Thou shalt safeguard thy fields from soil erosion, thy living waters from drying up, thy forests from desolation, and protect thy hills from overgrazing by the herds, that thy descendants may have abundance forever. If any shall fail in this stewardship of the land, thy fruitful fields shall become sterile stony ground or wasting gullies, and thy descendants shall decrease and live in poverty or perish from off the face of the earth."[5] Clearly, human beings were still at the forefront of Lowdermilk's concern. Yet, while regarding the

---

4. Ps. 104:14, 18.

5. "Walter C. Lowdermilk," Wikipedia, last modified August 30, 2018, https://en.wikipedia.org/wiki/Walter_C._Lowdermilk.

earth as a resource for bettering human life, he also understood that we cannot sustain and enrich the life of the human species unless we care for the rest of the creation.

Valid as Lowdermilk's concern is, I doubt that we need an eleventh commandment to make the point. It does not stretch the meaning of the second commandment, which forbids taking the Lord's name in vain, to see in it a warning against trying magically or scientifically to control the natural world as if we ourselves could control the power of the divine name. And likewise, the third commandment, enjoining us to trust God to care for us even when we relinquish our own efforts at control one day each week, reminds us that we do not and should not live by dominion over nature alone. Luther's explanation of the first article of the Creed in his Small Catechism—"I believe that God has created me *together with* all that exists"—captures nicely the way in which a belief in God's special care for humanity need not lead us to suppose that he does not also care for the whole creation.[6]

God's special care for humanity is sheer grace. How should we fittingly respond to it? With joy in the gift of life God bestows on us and on others. With gratitude for one's own life and the lives of others. "Radically and basically all sin is simply ingratitude."[7] Hence, the commandment reminds us that God's special care for humanity ought to evoke in us similar care.

It is no surprise, therefore, that we are commanded not to kill. We should almost certainly take the commandment as forbidding murder, which is a narrower category than killing in general. It is clear that Israel's own legal structures could and

6. Robert Kolb and Timothy J. Wengert, eds., *The Book of Concord: The Confessions of the Evangelical Lutheran Church* (Minneapolis: Fortress, 2000), 354 (emphasis added).

7. Karl Barth, *Church Dogmatics* IV/1, ed. G. W. Bromiley and T. F. Torrance (Edinburgh: T&T Clark, 1956), 41.

did make something like this distinction. Thus, for example, in Exodus 21 (the chapter that follows the giving of the Decalogue) the law distinguishes between one who "lies in wait" and kills another, and one who kills but did not lie in wait. It was for the protection of those who killed unintentionally that the law provided for cities of refuge.[8] These were places of sanctuary, given to protect "the manslayer who kills any person without intent" against private vengeance. This suggests that there might be killing that does not violate the commandment, a possibility to which we will return.

First, though, we should note that, because God makes the gift of life to each of us, we have a duty to respect not only the lives of others but also our own. Therefore, the church has generally taught that deliberate taking of one's own life is sin. This does not mean, it is important to note, that a person may not sacrifice his life for the sake of others or in the service of some great good. Knowingly to risk one's life in order to aim at an important good is not at all the same as deliberately taking aim at one's own life. Indeed, it is part of the glory of our human nature that we are able to rise above the mere animal instinct for self-preservation in order to serve others.

Deliberately taking one's own life is quite a different matter. Nevertheless, the very grandeur of the act and the nobility of some of its defenders (the ancient Stoics, for example) may invite us to suppose that such an exercise of freedom displays what is noblest in our humanity. Thus, without approving it, Bonhoeffer characterizes suicide as "a specifically human action" that refuses to bend the knee before "the blind inhuman force of destiny." He is not surprised, then, that it has "repeatedly been applauded and justified by noble human minds."[9] Nevertheless,

8. Cf. Num. 35:9–15.
9. Dietrich Bonhoeffer, *Ethics* (New York: Macmillan, 1955), 167.

he sees in it the paradigmatic temptation to "be like God," our own attempt "to give a final human meaning to a life which has become inhumanly meaningless."[10]

There may be exceptional cases in which the prohibition of suicide should be qualified. Both Barth and Bonhoeffer, for example, suggest that there could be instances in which a captive has to take his own life in order not to betray others by giving way under torture.[11] If, as I will suggest later, it is sometimes permissible to kill some neighbors in order to protect others who are in danger, it may also be that the neighbor who must sometimes be targeted in order to protect others is oneself. And, as Barth notes, Samson, who brings his own destruction upon himself in order to execute God's judgment upon the Philistines, is named in Hebrews 11:32 among the great cloud of witnesses from whom Christians are to take encouragement.[12]

But to spend too much time pondering the rare exceptional circumstance is to tempt ourselves into forgetting the prohibition, which must be taken with the utmost seriousness. To take it seriously, of course, need not mean supposing that one who takes his own life is necessarily separated from God and lost forever. The act that from our perspective writes *finis* to one's life may not be determinative in God's eyes. Bonhoeffer rightly says that the simple fact that one who commits suicide has no opportunity to repent does not settle the question of that person's eternal destiny. "Many Christians have died sudden deaths without having repented of all their sins. This is setting too much store by the last moment of life."[13] More decisive still, we should never deceive ourselves into supposing we can understand the depths

---

10. Bonhoeffer, *Ethics*, 167.
11. Bonhoeffer, *Ethics*, 171; Barth, *Church Dogmatics* III/4, ed. G. W. Bromiley and T. F. Torrance, trans. A. T. Mackay et al. (Edinburgh: T&T Clark, 1961), 412.
12. Cf. Judg. 16:30, where Samson says, "Let me die with the Philistines."
13. Bonhoeffer, *Ethics*, 169.

of the grace of a God with whom, as St. Paul says, "it is always Yes" (2 Cor. 1:19). Faith can hope for what sight cannot discern. Because, as St. John writes (John 1:5), "the light shines in the darkness, and the darkness has not overcome it," we should take seriously the psalmist's confidence:

> If I say, "Let only darkness cover me,
>   and the light about me be night,"
> even the darkness is not dark to thee,
>   the night is bright as the day;
>   for darkness is as light with thee. (Ps. 139:11–12)

Still, the prohibition of suicide matters. The more I begin to think of my life as mine to take if I wish, or the more willing I am to judge whether my life continues to have a point or is worth preserving, the more I may also be tempted to make similar judgments about others' lives—even to suppose that in so doing I exercise and display compassion. And in our current cultural climate, advocates of assisted suicide and euthanasia press that view relentlessly. They offer essentially two different sorts of argument, one grounded in self-determination, the other in compassion.

We find it quite natural to think to ourselves and say to others, "This is *my* life. Why shouldn't I be able to do with it as I please, so long of course as I hurt no one else in the process? I have been making important decisions about my life for years. Why should I not now be able to decide that my life is no longer worth sustaining, that I need to find someone willing and able to help me end it?" Surely we can understand how someone—especially someone in a society as individualistic as ours—might come to feel and think this way.

Nevertheless, the basic premise—the idea that I may do whatever I want with my life—is not really true. There are many things—including things that harm no one else—that even our relatively secular society will not authorize me to do. I may not ingest certain drugs, sell myself into slavery, marry my sister, engage in a duel, and so forth. No one really thinks I am entirely free to do with my life as I please. A young woman, referring to a cousin of hers who had committed suicide and to the effect it had on his family, once said, "He didn't just take his own life; he took part of theirs as well." He was not—and we are not—as independent of others and self-determining as we like to suppose. Our lives are always connected to others—as connected as we were at the beginning by the umbilical cord that sustained us. If we can see this much simply by the light of reason, how much more ought Christians, who know that the Author of our being has authority over us, bear witness against euthanasia and assisted suicide.

The other claim, that compassion should move us to endorse euthanasia, really means by "compassion" something that is a pale—and false—imitation of genuine Christian compassion. Our compassion for one another ought to be the compassion of *equals*, those who share equally the life bond to which the fifth commandment points. Genuine compassion is grounded in the fact that we do not make one another. Who does? Well, God does. Or even, for those who lack such faith, Nature does. But we are equals because none of us is the life-giver. I am not authorized to say that the time has come to snuff out your life. And you should not think you can give ultimate authority over your life to me.

Thus, although compassion surely moves us to try to relieve the suffering of others, there are still things we ought not do even for the sake of that worthy end—things that would not suit our shared human condition. There may be some suffering that must be accepted and endured—suffered—because we can find no right way to relieve it entirely. Hence, the virtue of compassion has a shape and has limits; it is not just a formless emotion. The imperative that should guide our care of others is not "minimize suffering," but "maximize care." Quite often these will come to the same thing, but not always. It is not our task to judge whether our life or the life of another still has meaning and purpose. It is our task to relieve whatever suffering we rightly can and to keep company with those whose suffering we cannot relieve entirely.

We should not end this discussion of the life bond in the light of creation without reminding ourselves that we read the commandment too narrowly if we think of it simply in negative terms, as prohibiting various kinds of killing. So, for example, in the Small Catechism's explanation of the fifth commandment, Luther writes, "We should fear and love God, and so we should not endanger our neighbor's life, nor cause him any harm, but help and befriend him in every necessity of life."[14] To take this seriously is to realize that avoiding forbidden forms of killing is by no means the extent of what the life bond asks of us. Many who would never be tempted to kill (or even hate) may neglect the needs of others. To be sure, there will always be more human need than any of us is able to meet, and we differ in our capacity to offer care and help, but if we do not help and befriend those in need when and where we are able, we fall short of what our created fellow humanity asks of us.

The Life Bond in Need of Healing

In Jesus of Nazareth, God stands beside us. Sharing the common bond of life he gave us as our Creator, he comes to renew

14. Theodore Tappert, ed., *The Book of Concord* (Philadelphia: Muhlenberg, 1959), 343.

a world distorted by human sin. Nevertheless, although the Spirit of Christ has already been given as a guarantee of the promised redemption yet to come, it is still true that the whole creation—ourselves included—remains in need of healing and must for a time live in expectation of what has been promised.[15] For now, therefore, God's "yes" to us will not always be apparent. In order to preserve the world toward the new creation, God's care and concern for us may take a puzzling form in the work of government.

When human life is threatened, God intervenes to protect those who are endangered, passing judgment on wrong and punishing wrongdoers. Of course, God does this not with lightning bolts from heaven but, rather, through human agents and institutions—that is, through government and its officials. Within the Bible it is the opening verses of Romans 13 that most clearly articulate this.

> Let every person be subject to the governing authorities. For there is no authority except from God, and those that exist have been instituted by God. . . . For rulers are not a terror to good conduct, but to bad. Would you have no fear of him who is in authority? Then do what is good, and you will receive his approval, for he is God's servant for your good. But if you do wrong, be afraid, for he does not bear the sword in vain; he is the servant of God to execute his wrath on the wrongdoer. (vv. 1, 3–4)

If we attend to the context of these verses, we will note that this judicial and retributive function is granted not to individuals in their private capacities but to government.

Immediately before the opening verses of Romans 13, St. Paul makes clear that Christians should not return evil for evil. "Do not be overcome by evil," he writes, "but overcome evil with

15. 2 Cor. 1:22; 5:5; Rom. 8:18–25.

good" (Rom. 12:21).[16] And having briefly described government's retributive work as God's own preserving of the world, Paul returns to the theme of love in 13:8: "Owe no one anything, except to love one another."

When we place the description of government's work within this context, it is clear that Paul himself thinks that God's judicial and retributive work through the institutions of government is strange, veiling the "yes" he always speaks in what looks all too much like a "no." But nevertheless, Paul says, strange as it may seem, we who are taught not to live by the law of retribution where our own interests are concerned should recognize that government carries out its retributive work as God's servant. To be sure, Paul does not go on to say that Christians should themselves participate in exercising governmental power. On that point, however, we may well quote Luther, who sees the issue clearly: "Be not so wicked, my friend, as to say, 'A Christian may not do that which is God's own peculiar work, ordinance, and creation.' . . . If it is God's work and creation, then it is good, so good that everyone can use it in a Christian and salutary way."[17] Thus, what we ought not do simply to protect our own interests we may and should do to protect the interests of others. Such protection is precisely the work of government. "Although you do not need to have your enemy punished, your afflicted neighbor does."[18] God so orders human life that, as Charles Williams memorably puts it, "no man can paddle his own canoe and every man can paddle his fellow's."[19]

We see God's work of judgment, retribution, and protection daily in those who exercise the police power in our society. Even

16. My interpretation will largely follow Oscar Cullmann, *The State in the New Testament* (New York: Scribner's Sons, 1956), chap. 3.

17. Luther, "Temporal Authority: To What Extent It Should Be Obeyed," in *Luther's Works* (Philadelphia: Muhlenberg, 1962), 45:99.

18. Luther, "Temporal Authority," 95.

19. Charles Williams, *Arthurian Torso* (London: Oxford, 1948), 123.

more strikingly, however, we see it on those more rare occasions
when governments wage war. Far more has been written about
the moral problems raised by warfare than we can examine. Here
I will make just three important points, developing only the third
of them in some detail.

We need, first, to take stock of our obligations within a world
deeply scarred by sin. The historian Herbert Butterfield is sup-
posed to have said that if we take the animosity present in an
average church choir and give that animosity a history by extend-
ing it over time, we will have an adequate explanation of all the
wars ever fought in human history. His point was simple, and it is
the first point we need to make here: we are not going to be able
to eliminate hostility and warfare from human history. If not,
what then? We could just throw our hands up, accepting the fact
that every political community must do whatever is necessary
to preserve its way of life. By contrast, the attempt to formulate
criteria by which to determine the justice of war is an attempt
to keep war a limited, moral activity. It enacts a refusal to believe
that we are entirely at the mercy of our desires and fears.

To be sure, throughout the history of the church some Christians have responded to war's destructiveness with the claim
that—whatever others may say or do—those who follow Christ
should be opposed to all war and committed to pacifism. There
have always been differences in Christian opinion and practice,
but pacifism has been a recurring tendency, especially strong at
certain times and places: among believers in the first century who
opposed the emperor worship required in the Roman army at
least as much as they opposed waging war; among some Christians in the Middle Ages who did not believe that shedding blood
could be compatible with the holiness Christ asked of his followers; among some (such as Mennonites) in the sixteenth century
who were part of what has come to be called the left wing of the
Reformation; among Quakers in seventeenth-century England;

and, in more recent times, among some Christians for whom the destructive power of modern weapons makes pacifism obligatory for believers, whether or not it was in earlier times.

Christian pacifists are not simply opposed to the use of force, but, more positively, they are committed to the belief that we can trust God to care for his creation. Leaving that to God, we are then called simply to heed the voice of Jesus, who says, "Do not resist one who is evil" (Matt. 5:39). The difficulty Christian pacifists always face, however, is that they risk seeming indifferent to the claims of justice, all too willing to permit injustice to continue. God cares for the world and for those facing danger precisely through the work of government—sometimes, even, through the use of force. Supporting this work of government and participating in it is not a failure to trust God; rather, it expresses our belief that God works through the institutions of government. Here we might recall again Luther's point. What we ought not do in our own defense we may be called to do in the defense of a neighbor in need. Strangely enough, therefore, even warfare itself can sometimes be a work of love.

To develop moral criteria by which to govern war is not to deny its horrors or destructiveness. It is simply to believe that even if war is hell, our task is, as Michael Walzer once put it, to carve out "a constitutional regime" in hell.[20] The criteria governing warfare have generally been of two kinds, and that is the second point worth noting here. Some criteria govern the justice of going to war in the first place. Others concern what is permitted within the conduct of war (whether or not one's decision to wage war in the first place had been a just one). The two sorts of criteria are not unrelated. We may permissibly begin to wage war if there is no other way to try to achieve a just and lasting peace. But then we can hardly wage war in a manner so

20. Michael Walzer, *Just and Unjust Wars* (New York: Basic Books, 1977), 40.

unrestrained that it destroys any chance of actually achieving such a just, enduring social order.

Central to the decision even to begin to wage war is the need for "just cause." In recent times there has been an increasing tendency to argue that there can be only one just cause—namely, defense against an aggressor. Hence, on that view it could never be right to strike first, and there could be no such thing as a just aggressive war. To be sure, there are good reasons to hesitate before expanding the concept of just cause beyond defense against aggression, especially when we consider that nation-states are all too eager to cloak their aggressive policies beneath humanitarian claims. And, even if their motives are not sullied in this way, government officials can easily overestimate their ability to reshape the world for the better. Still, granting all those good reasons for caution, we would be mistaken to rule out the very possibility of warfare intended not for our own defense but to uphold the claims—and the lives—of those who are being terribly wronged. And, in fact, only in relatively recent times have Christians thought otherwise. We would do well to reclaim the older, more expansive understanding of just cause.

A third point that needs attention here is perhaps the most complicated. To wage war justly must always be a limited undertaking, even if—perhaps especially if—our cause is clearly just and may therefore tempt us to do whatever is needed to succeed. And the chief limitation on the waging of war is the requirement that only combatants—not civilians and not soldiers who have surrendered—may be the objects of direct, intended attack. It is not because they are especially evil that combatants may be attacked. Indeed, many civilians may be more eager for war than the soldiers who are their fellow citizens. But soldiers may be attacked because they are not "innocent" in a technical sense. They are those whose actions threaten immediate harm to others, and therefore they may be opposed and targeted.

In most combat situations, however, no matter how scrupu-
lously combatants target only other combatants and the ma-
terials they need to wage war, it is likely that some civilians will
be killed or injured—not because they were targeted, but simply
because such collateral harm is often a by-product of military
strikes aimed justly at legitimate targets. Notice that we may
well foresee the likelihood of such unintended harm to noncom-
batants; yet, that does not mean war has been waged unjustly.

To see why this is true we need to distinguish between what
we *do* and what is *accomplished* by our doing. Most of the time,
even though we may have a very particular aim in acting, that
action is likely to produce several results, some good and some
evil. And quite often we may foresee that what we do is likely to
result not only in the good at which we aim but also in evils we
do not intend and would regret. In a world that still needs healing, we cannot eliminate all such evils, but we can take care not
to make them our aim. The concept of foreseen but unintended
effect—distinguishing evils that, so to speak, accompany our
action from evils we embrace—is crucial for moral reasoning. It
distinguishes evil that is a by-product of setting out to seek the
good from evil with which we invest the personal involvement
of our purpose. Without such a distinction, anyone able and
willing to threaten foreseeable, sufficiently evil results will be
in a position to obligate us to act in whatever way he requires.
Realizing this, we might even say that distinguishing what we
do from foreseeable results of our action is necessary if we are
to be free from moral coercion.

This is not just a point about morality; it is a point about what
it means to be creatures whose love and care for others must
always be love and care within limits. From a purely impersonal
standpoint our actions might be regarded just as events in the
world. But as moral agents—as creatures made for communion
in love with God, and creatures whose character is shaped in

action—we can never so regard them. Our actions are not simply
events in the world; they are occasions in which, so to speak, we
come upon ourselves and learn at least in part who we are. To
aim at evil, even in a good cause, is to take into our person a
choice against what is good—not just to let evil happen, but to
give it the personal involvement of our purpose. Put in Christian
terms, it is to begin to make of ourselves people who would not
want to be with God.

Sometimes we may be uncertain how to make these distinctions, how to sort out the complications presented by difficult
circumstances. That is one reason why moral judgments may not
always be easily transferrable to a court of law. But the fact that
some of these cases are hard does not mean we should not draw
the distinctions as best we can. Ignoring the complications may
seem to simplify matters, but it will be a simplicity that misses
much of moral importance.

There is in the Bible another and different perspective on the
conduct of war—a perspective sometimes called "holy war." It
plays a central role in Israel's conquest of the promised land, at
least as that conquest is depicted in the book of Joshua. (The
depiction in the book of Judges is rather different.) This perspective is programmatically articulated in Moses' instructions
to Israel (in the book of Deuteronomy) when Israel is about to
enter the land to possess it. Against cities that opposed Israel as
they made their way toward Canaan, the instructions had been
somewhat different (and, we could say, milder). Israel was to
"offer terms of peace." If the terms were accepted, they could
then put the inhabitants of the city to forced labor. If the terms
were not accepted, they could lay siege to the city, put all its
male citizens to death, and take its women, children, and cattle
as the spoils of war.[21]

21. Deut. 20:10–15.

But with respect to cities occupying the land that Israel had been promised by God and was about to enter, Moses' instructions were more far-reaching and included a justifying reason for what was commanded. Israel was to execute a sacred "ban" of all people and valued objects in the enemy's cities. "In the cities of these peoples that the LORD your God gives you for an inheritance, you shall save alive nothing that breathes, but you shall utterly destroy them, the Hittites and the Amorites, the Canaanites and the Perizzites, the Hivites and the Jebusites, as the LORD your God has commanded; that they may not teach you to do according to all their abominable practices which they have done in the service of their gods, and so to sin against the LORD your God" (Deut. 20:16–18). Deeply troubling as such passages are, one thing is clear: these directives are limited quite specifically to Israel's conquest of the land. They have no application in other times and places.

What else, if anything, can we say to try to come to terms with these passages? One thing we know is that waging a war of extermination was not unique to Israel at the time. More than a century ago a stone inscribed in the Phoenician alphabet and known now as the Moabite stone was discovered in what is modern-day Jordan. In the fragments that remain, the Moabite king Mesha recounts a directive he received from Moab's god Chemosh concerning the prosecution of his war with Israel: "And Chemosh said to me, 'Go, take Nebo against Israel.' And I went by night and fought against it from the break of dawn till noon; and I took it and slew all: seven thousand men, boys, women, and [girls,] and female slaves, for I had consecrated it to Ashtar-Chemosh."[22] This, it seems, is the way wars sometimes were

---

22. James B. Pritchard, ed., *The Ancient Near East: An Anthology of Texts and Pictures* (Princeton: Princeton University Press, 1958), 209–10, quoted in Michael Walzer, *In God's Shadow: Politics in the Hebrew Bible* (New Haven and London: Yale University Press, 2012), 35.

fought both by Israel and by other peoples at the time. For God to elect Israel as his peculiar people and give them the land he had promised required a willingness to be Lord of history not in some fictional world but in the world Israel actually inhabited.

The justifying reason given in Deuteronomy 20, cited above, which clearly sets the "ban" in the context of Israel's conquest of Canaan, also has to do with Israel's special status as God's elect people. The suggestion is that, if the other peoples are allowed to live alongside Israel, it is likely that their idolatrous practices will corrupt Israelite religious life and worship. Hence, in order that (as God had promised Abram) all the peoples of the earth may be blessed through Israel, idolatry must be kept at a distance. Israel must remain narrow in order to be a light to the nations. None of these considerations is likely to silence our uneasiness when we read these stories, but they do amplify and complicate the picture in ways we should not fail to see.

We know, of course, from the accounts in the book of Judges that Israel clearly did not exterminate the other peoples of the land.[23] The process of settlement recounted in Judges is slower and considerably less decisive, which suggests that we should read the accounts in Joshua as a radically foreshortened and telescoped account of what Israel believed God would do in order to keep his promise to Abram. In any case, this holy war tradition cannot guide our moral thinking in other times and places, for the nation-states we inhabit are not the elect people of Israel.

Of course, waging war is not the only way in which government bears the sword. Its work of judgment and retribution

---

23. This despite a summary passage such as the following from Josh. 11:18–20: "Joshua made war a long time with all those kings. There was not a city that made peace with the people of Israel, except the Hivites, the inhabitants of Gibeon; they took all in battle. For it was the LORD's doing to harden their hearts that they should come against Israel in battle, in order that they should be utterly destroyed, and should receive no mercy but be exterminated, as the LORD commanded Moses."

is exercised not only against external enemies but also against lawbreakers who are members of a society. No doubt this work of punishment is not always carried out justly, but in many instances it is a rightful exercise of authority by rulers who are, as Romans 13 puts it, a terror not to good but to bad conduct. One very special case, however, which clearly forces us to think about the life bond to which the fifth commandment points, is capital punishment.

One of the scriptural passages that has been significant in shaping the church's traditional position on the death penalty is Genesis 9:6, which reads, "Whoever sheds the blood of man, by man shall his blood be shed; for God made man in his own image." This passage comes after the story of Noah and the great flood. The covenant that God makes with humankind then takes into account the fact of human sinfulness. Therefore, although God promises never again to send such a flood upon the earth, he authorizes the use of force—even killing—in order to preserve a sinful world toward the day, soon to begin with the call of Abram, when he will save in a new way.

There is, however, something strange about all this. On the one hand, because human beings are made in God's image, they are not to be killed. But, on the other hand, one who sheds another's blood may—and perhaps should—himself be executed. Doesn't that, we might ask, simply repeat the wrong? One human being, mistakenly supposing that he is lord over another's life, sheds that person's blood. And now other human beings are prepared to shed his blood in turn, as if they were lords over his life. Natural as such a question may seem to us, there is no paradox here if we remember the teaching of Romans 13 that government carries out its task of judgment and retribution as God's servant. When properly constituted government officials execute a murderer, theirs is not an act of private vengeance, nor does it mean that they are exercising lordship over the life of a fellow human being. For they act not as private avengers but in a public capacity. Not as private individuals but as representatives of public justice. Thus, what happens is not that some human beings exercise lordship over the life of another. Rather, the true Lord of life and death carries out his judgment through the hands of human beings.

Of course, to say that government officials who judge and punish wrongdoers act as God's representatives does not mean that their judgment must take the form of the death penalty. It does, however, help to explain why, with relatively few exceptions until recent times, the tradition of the church has accepted the authority of the state to execute wrongdoers—even while quite often combining that with the belief that Christians (or, at least, Christian clergy) should always support mercy and clemency for those sentenced to die. We might say that the church has simply acknowledged the permissibility of the death penalty without necessarily encouraging or cheering its use.

Increasingly we find Christians drawing back from all support for the death penalty. Perhaps the most striking example has been the steady movement in official Roman Catholic teaching. Without precisely arguing for abolition, the *Catechism of the Catholic Church* has taught that, at least in a developed country such as the United States, there may never be circumstances in which capital punishment is needed (or, therefore, permissible).[24] What would seem to be the final step in that movement came in 2018 when Pope Francis revised the *Catechism* so that it now teaches that the death penalty is "inadmissible."[25] Here I will not attempt to examine in detail this changed emphasis, but it

24. This is especially true of the 1997 revisions to the text of the *Catechism*.
25. "New Revision of Number 2267 of the *Catechism of the Catholic Church* on the Death Penalty—Rescriptum 'Ex Audientia SS.MI'," The Vatican, accessed August 5, 2019, http://www.vatican.va/roman_curia/congregations/cfaith/documents/rc_con_cfaith_doc_20180801_catechismo-penadimorte_en.html.

is important to consider carefully one issue. The problem is not that the Roman Catholic Church may cease to support the death penalty. As I said, we need hardly be cheerleaders for capital punishment. The problem is that the argument for abolition is in danger of taking a form that undercuts the legitimacy of government's authority to judge and punish—a legitimacy that goes very deep into Christian history and thought.

The *Catechism* treats the death penalty under the heading of "legitimate defense," not under a heading such as "the authority of government to punish and execute wrongdoers." Placing the discussion within a context of "legitimate defense" tends to conflate government's action with what any of us might do as a private individual. Even when private individuals are entitled to defend themselves or others against those threatening immediate harm, they are not authorized to judge and punish the evildoers. But when government officials judge and punish, they do not defend or avenge themselves. They render public judgment, acting on behalf of the entire community and mediating God's own judgment on wrongdoing. Hence, what would be wrong for any of us to do in our private capacity may not be wrong for those acting in government's public capacity.

Thus, the real danger is not that individual Christians or the church may come to argue for elimination of the death penalty. Although that would be a break with the tradition of the church, it is surely a matter about which believers might disagree. The real danger is that we may forget that punishment is an aspect of government's authority to judge. To lose the distinction between public and private is to begin to lose a theory of government's distinctive authority as God's servant.

On the traditional view, which the church taught for centuries, the criminal may be executed as an appropriate judgment on the evil he has done—even though he is no longer a threat to anyone. It is not a matter of defense but of the authority granted government to judge and punish in order to sustain the common life of its people. And the death penalty, if it is exacted, should not be understood as inflicting on the criminal a punishment similar to the evil he has done. (We do not punish rapists by raping them.) What the convicted criminal receives is, in Oliver O'Donovan's perceptive phrase, "not an echo but an answer. More precisely, it is a 'judgment.'"[26] Civil government responds to his crime not by retaliating but by pronouncing judgment—giving to the offender "a truthful response to the offense."[27] That is what government, as God's servant, is and does.

Having attended to issues such as warfare and punishment, we should recall that the healing our world needs quite often involves just that: the healing of illness and disease. Clearly, human life east of Eden is marked by illness and fragility. While it is true, as Barth writes, that "life is no second God," it is equally true, as he also writes, that sickness "is an encroachment on the life which God has created."[28] Hence, although we do not approve either euthanasia or suicide, we should try to relieve suffering and serve the good of health in ourselves and others. Characterizing the mandate to heal within the Jewish tradition, David Feldman writes, "Though God is master of both life and death, good and evil, we are partners with Him only in the bias for life. We imitate only His attribute of mercy, and the ethical imperative moves us to advance the cause of life and health."[29] Surely, then, we who believe that, in Jesus, God has shared the bond of life with us and healed disease as a sign of the renewed creation still to come should likewise be committed to the mandate to heal where we

26. Oliver O'Donovan, *The Ways of Judgment* (Grand Rapids: Eerdmans, 2005), 110.

27. O'Donovan, *Ways of Judgment*, 113.

28. Barth, *Church Dogmatics* III/4, 342, 366.

29. David M. Feldman, *Health and Medicine in the Jewish Tradition* (New York: Crossroad, 1986), 19.

can and to comfort the sick even when we cannot heal. Setting our face against illness, we rightly honor the medical profession and its commitment to healing.

This does not mean that we must always do everything within our power to keep one who is ill alive. We should always choose life, not death, but the life we choose need not be the longest one available. Refusing or withdrawing life-prolonging treatment when it is either useless or excessively burdensome has been considered good medicine for centuries. One may rightly choose a life that is free of burdensome treatments, even if it is also somewhat shorter than might be possible; hence, death need not always be opposed. Refusing to kill does not mean doing everything within our power to extend life. But we should choose life, even if sometimes that only means how to live while dying.

The Life Bond and the Promised Redemption

While sickness is an encroachment on the gift of life, aging is itself a part of the life each of us is given. We live in time, and its movement should remind us that we live toward a destiny that remains as mysterious as God is mysterious. Citing Aquinas, Josef Pieper writes, "A being obviously directed toward something else 'cannot possibly have as his ultimate goal the preservation of his own existence.' In other words, the allaying of the thirst cannot consist simply in the mere continued existence of the thirster."[30] We are made for something more than this created life—made not simply to "see in a mirror dimly," but "face to face." Made to "understand fully," even as we "have been fully understood."[31]

30. Josef Pieper, *Happiness and Contemplation* (South Bend, IN: St. Augustine's Press, 1998), 36.
31. 1 Cor. 13:12.

Then, when thirst has been satisfied, we will know that "joy is the serious business of Heaven."[32]

That day is not yet, however. Unless we are among those still living when the risen Lord returns in glory, we will have to make our way to that day through death. And it is in the funeral service, the rite of Christian burial, that we honor to the end the created life bond, a bond the incarnate Son of God has shared with us. We need, therefore, to think briefly about what that funeral service should be and do, for its significance is increasingly obscured in our world. Simply put, Christians should do what the title of Thomas Long's book-length discussion of the Christian funeral urges: *Accompany Them with Singing.*[33]

A Christian funeral is not a memorial service, not a celebration of life, not an occasion for eulogizing the deceased—any and all of which can be and often are done without the presence of the dead body. "A good funeral transports the newly deceased and the newly bereaved to the borders of a changed reality. The dead are disposed of in a way that says they mattered to us, and the living are brought to the edge of a life they will lead without the one who has died. We deal with death by dealing with the dead, not just the idea but also the sad and actual fact of the matter—the dead body."[34] After all, the entire Christian life is a pilgrimage, a journey that begins in baptism and moves toward the new creation that the risen Christ now lives and promises will be ours. We who have accompanied a deceased person along this way, and certainly those of us who have been loved ones and fellow believers, ought not cut the journey short. "This saint, though deceased, is still joined to the congregation and

32. C. S. Lewis, *Letters to Malcolm: Chiefly on Prayer* (New York: Harcourt, Brace & World, 1964), 93.

33. Thomas G. Long, *Accompany Them with Singing—The Christian Funeral* (Louisville: Westminster John Knox, 2009).

34. Thomas Lynch, "Good Grief," *Christian Century* 120 (July 26, 2003), 20.

is coming in the body to this place one last time for worship."[35] Hence, when that service is ended we make one more journey together—to the place of burial—accompanying the dead body as far as we are able.

There are reasons to think that, although cremation of the dead body is not in itself wrong, burial in the ground is likely to capture better the Christian significance of death. The dead body, St. Paul writes, "is sown in weakness, it is raised in power. It is sown a physical body, it is raised a spiritual body" (1 Cor. 15:43–44). Burying seeds in the earth in the hope that a power greater than ours will bring new life from those buried seeds is an essential human activity. And so we place the bodies of our dead in the ground, in the hope that in his own time God will give them new life.

Cremation is more likely than burial to invite us to think in terms of a memorial service rather than a funeral service. Then the focus is less on accompanying the dead person to the very end of his or her earthly journey than on the feelings and emotions of the mourners. Even more important, the absence of a dead body almost inevitably suggests to us that the body is a mere, dispensable husk, not the kernel, not the place of the person's presence. And then, in turn, we are likely to suppose that the dead person has already attained the fullness of what God promises—since, after all, the memorial service is his or her "victory celebration"—and no resurrection of the body is needed to make the victory complete.

"How is it," Thomas Lynch asks, "that so many people claim a preference for cremation but so few have any interest in knowing more about it?"[36] This suggests that if Christians complete their journey with cremation rather than burial, we the living

35. Long, *Accompany Them with Singing*, 154.
36. Thomas Lynch, "The Holy Fire," *Christian Century* 127 (April 6, 2010), 23.

should accompany them to the crematorium even as we do to the cemetery. As Lynch puts it, we need to treat cremation "as an alternative to burial, rather than an alternative to bother."[37] The life bond is a bond we share in our bodies—bodies that we believe will one day be raised with Christ in the new creation. The last stage of our earthly pilgrimage should bear witness to that hope.

We cannot say much about what the redeemed life we are promised will be like. Quite rightly, in fact, C. S. Lewis suggests that "the task of the imagination here is not to forecast it but simply . . . to make room for a more complete and circumspect agnosticism."[38] What we should not do is picture the life of the new creation in vaguely spiritual terms; for, as surely as Christ is risen, that new life will be an embodied one. "Our conception of Heaven as *merely* a state of mind is not unconnected with the fact that the specifically Christian virtue of Hope has in our time grown so languid. Where our fathers, peering into the future, saw gleams of gold, we see only the mist, white, featureless, cold and never moving."[39]

One thing about the redeemed life God promises *is* certain. By the power of the Spirit of the risen Christ, we will be perfect as our heavenly Father is perfect (Matt. 5:48). For the moment, we may be tempted to think of this simply as a command, something we are to accomplish. But when we understand fully as we have been fully understood, we will come to see that it is a promise— the promise of a genuinely redeemed life in which there will no longer be any need to distinguish enemies from friends, since in that day no enemies will remain for us.

37. Lynch, "Holy Fire," 26.
38. C. S. Lewis, *Miracles* (New York: Macmillan, 1947), 158.
39. Lewis, *Miracles*, 168.

❧ CHAPTER 5 ❧

The Possessions Bond

You shall not steal.
You shall not covet your neighbor's house; you shall not covet
your neighbor's wife, or his manservant, or his maidservant, or
his ox, or his ass, or anything that is your neighbor's.
Remember the sabbath day, to keep it holy.

Exodus 20:15, 17, 8

Probably the most puzzling sections of Jesus' Sermon on the
Mount are the "antitheses" of Matthew 5, where the bonds that
connect our lives are intensified almost beyond our bearing. The
life bond is there: We're told, and we can understand, that murder is wrong. But, Jesus says, don't even be angry with another.
The marriage bond is there: We're told, and we can understand,
that adultery is wrong. But, Jesus says, even lustful desire for
another's spouse is forbidden. The speech bond is there: We're
told, and we can understand, that swearing falsely is wrong.
But, Jesus says, any swearing at all must be avoided. The family
bond is there, although we have to stretch a bit to see it: We're

told, and we can understand, that we should love those who are
nearest to us. But, Jesus says, we should love not only those who
love us, but even and also our enemies.

The possessions bond, however, is mostly absent from the
famous antitheses of chapter 5. We can create our own somewhat
different kind of antithesis by beginning with words recorded
in chapter 6: "Do not lay up for yourselves treasures on earth,
where moth and rust consume and where thieves break in and
steal, but lay up for yourselves treasures in heaven, where neither
moth nor rust consumes and where thieves do not break in and
steal. For where your treasure is, there will your heart be also"
(Matt. 6:19–21). Handle the things of this world rightly, Jesus
says, and your heart will be trained to love God. Clean up what
is outside, and your inner character will be rightly shaped. A
few chapters later, however, Jesus seems to suggest the opposite
direction of movement: get the inner spirit right, and you'll have
no problem with external possessions. "Either make the tree
good, and its fruit good; or make the tree bad, and its fruit bad;
for the tree is known by its fruit. . . . The good man out of his
good treasure brings forth good, and the evil man out of his evil
treasure brings forth evil" (Matt. 12:33, 35).

A similar contrast is present in the Beatitudes. In Matthew
(5:3) Jesus says, "Blessed are the poor in spirit, for theirs is
the kingdom of heaven." Possessions themselves do not seem
to be a problem so long as one's spirit is rightly ordered. The
focus is on that inner spirit, not on the amount of one's possessions. But the parallel passage—which is not so parallel!—in
Luke (6:20) reverses the focal point: "Blessed are you poor, for
yours is the kingdom of God." Poverty itself is praised as an
ideal. Clearly, Christians will need to say more than one thing
about ways in which possessions bind together human lives.
The most basic truth, however, was enunciated long ago by
an Israelite sage: "The rich and the poor meet together; / the

LORD is the maker of them all" (Prov. 22:2). If they do not yet "meet together" in our world, the history of redemption must not yet be complete.

The Possessions Bond in Creation

The good things of creation are given for our pleasure and enjoyment. Hence, we do no wrong when we acquire them, care about them, and delight in them. Nevertheless, it is still true that these good gifts are *created* things. We see them for what they really are only if we allow them to call us out of ourselves, seeing in them hints of the Creator's goodness and glory. This means that our love for the things we have should never be characterized in only one way. Certainly we are to enjoy them. But we must also turn from them to the One who gives them. After all, the goodness we see in our possessions is not simply *in* them; it comes to us *through* them. We can rightly say, then, that their created character should invite us to enjoy them and, simultaneously, nudge us to turn from love for them to their Creator. The Christian life is neither simply enjoyment of possessions nor renunciation of them; it involves a constant movement between enjoyment and renunciation, because created things are not Goodness itself. To be sure, some of us may need to be encouraged to renounce possessions more than we do, while others of us may need to learn to take greater pleasure in the gifts of the Creator. But for all of us it is likely to be true that neither half of that dialectical movement, taken by itself, can possibly be adequate.

Of course, we live in a world whose economic structures are less likely to encourage renunciation than they are the desire to acquire possessions—and then still more possessions. But a desire for gain is not in itself forbidden by the commandments

that prohibit stealing and coveting.[1] Avarice, a desire that cannot
be sated or satisfied, is forbidden, but that is a distortion of the
desire for gain. Not money but the love of money is the root of
all kinds of evil.[2] The commandments prohibit cheating others
or stealing from them and require us to help others who are in
need. It is also true, however, that we are in the world as people
with projects and plans, and most of the time this means we
must acquire possessions in order to carry out those projects. It
cannot be wrong to want such possessions.

Nevertheless, we should be careful not to congratulate ourselves too quickly on the goods we have acquired. Calvin reminds
us, "What every man possesses has not come to him by mere
chance but by the distribution of the supreme Lord of all."[3] That
means, as Calvin notes, that to take what belongs to someone else
is to set aside "God's dispensation." But it also means that from
our perspective there will always be something a little arbitrary
about the distribution of this world's goods; it is God's doing
and not simply ours. And so, if we have many possessions, we
probably have not managed that entirely on our own. The self-
made man is a myth.

We must, therefore, take seriously a distinction of the sort
Aquinas makes between the possession and the use of our goods.[4]
God gives us, St. Thomas says, the power "to procure and dispense" the good things of creation—in short, to own and use
them. Indeed, Thomas gives reasons why human life will be more
orderly and peaceful if a division of possessions—what we would

1. R. R. Reno, "God or Mammon," in *I Am the Lord Your God: Christian
Reflections on the Ten Commandments*, ed. Carl E. Braaten and Christopher R.
Seitz (Grand Rapids: Eerdmans, 2005), 218–36. Though helpful, the essay does not
always clearly distinguish a desire for gain from the vice of avarice.
2. 1 Tim. 6:10.
3. John Calvin, *Institutes of the Christian Religion*, ed. John T. McNeill, trans.
Ford Lewis Battles, Library of Christian Classics 20 (Philadelphia: Westminster,
1960), 2.8.45.
4. Cf. *Summa Theologiae* IIaIIae, q. 66, a. 2.

describe as private ownership—is recognized and honored. If, however, "possession" is private, the same is not entirely true of "use." We should, Thomas adds, think of our possessions not only as ours but also as held "in common." That is, we should be ready to share them with others who are in need, remembering that God first gave the good things of creation not to individuals but to humankind for our nourishment and delight. We should be guided by the understanding of equality that St. Paul recommends to the Corinthians—not that all should have the same amount of this world's goods, but that those who possess should share with those in need. "I do not mean that others should be eased and you burdened, but that as a matter of equality your abundance at the present time should supply their want, so that their abundance may supply your want, that there may be equality" (2 Cor. 8:13–14). That is, God has so arranged the world that "no man can paddle his own canoe and every man can paddle his fellow's."[5]

Therefore, the commandments that prohibit coveting and stealing, when taken seriously, penetrate deeply into our everyday lives. Luther's succinct explanation in his Small Catechism of the commandment that forbids stealing makes clear how far this reach extends. We are, in the first place, not to "take our neighbors' money or property." That alone, however, does not suffice. We should also not defraud neighbors by "using shoddy merchandise or crooked deals." Beyond these negative requirements there remains still a positive duty: to help our neighbors "to improve and protect their property and income."[6]

The commandments that forbid coveting another's possessions deal less with actions than with attitudes; hence, they seek to shape our character in far-reaching ways. The goods of another

5. Charles Williams, *Arthurian Torso* (London: Oxford, 1948), 123.
6. Robert Kolb and Timothy J. Wengert, eds., *The Book of Concord: The Confessions of the Evangelical Lutheran Church* (Minneapolis: Fortress, 2000), 353.

that we are not to covet include property (a house), people (wife and slaves), and the animals whose work helps to sustain human life. Our initial reaction is likely to be that classifying the neighbor's wife among his possessions is a relic of a culture we would rightly reject. Nonetheless, as Patrick Miller points out, we can also "hear in the commandment an understanding of possession that incorporates *personal relationships* as well as economic goods." What the neighbor possesses and what we might covet is a relationship that has not only economic importance but also personal significance—"a pointer to the way in which human possessions incorporate significant human relationships."[7]

To be sure, those who are poor, who have little opportunity to enjoy the gifts God gives in the creation, should not be told simply to be content with their lot in life. They are not wrong to want to enjoy a larger portion of the blessings of creation. Nonetheless, although we may rightly want a share in the neighbor's *goods*, we should not want *the neighbor's* goods. For all of us it is true that "there is great gain in godliness with contentment" (1 Tim. 6:6). In coveting we not only wrong others, we wrong ourselves. As William F. May notes, when I covet your good things, it's as if I ignore the time, the place, and the gifts given me. How can we say, "I wish I were in your shoes," while still being grateful for the gifts God has given us? "Grief for the good of another is blindness to the self's own treasure from God."[8] But when we turn to God with grateful hearts, the beauties of creation can also be ours to enjoy.

7. Patrick D. Miller, *The Ten Commandments* (Louisville: Westminster John Knox, 2009), 394. David Baker also notes that "whatever the precise social status of women may have been in ancient societies" such as Israel, a man's wife is not included in a list of possessions, for she was not regarded as "a saleable item." Cf. David L. Baker, *The Decalogue: Living as the People of God* (Downers Grove, IL: IVP Academic, 2017), 147.

8. William F. May, *A Catalogue of Sins* (New York: Holt, Rinehart and Winston, 1967), 79.

The Possessions Bond in Need of Healing

In the early stages of the monastic movement, sayings of the desert fathers were widely circulated. Among them is the following:

> Two old men lived together for many years without a quarrel. One said to the other: "Let us have one quarrel with each other, as is the way of men." And the other answered: "I do not know how a quarrel happens." And the first said: "Look, I put a tile between us, and I say, That's mine. Then you say, No, it's mine. That is how you begin a quarrel."
>
> So they put a tile between them, and one of them said: "That's mine." And the other said: "No, it's mine." And he answered: "Yes, it is yours. Take it away." And they went away unable to argue with each other.[9]

Of course, we know that disputes over property are not the only way to generate a quarrel, but it is no accident that one important target of the threefold monastic vow (of chastity, poverty, and obedience) was the human desire for possessions. Sensing how easily our anarchic desires (for sex, property, and power) could disrupt the peace of creation and turn the Creator's gifts into reasons for hostility, the monks took a path of what we might call heroic renunciation.

It is not clear, however, that the monastic movement ever really managed to solve the problem of possessions. As is well known, the history of monasticism in the Middle Ages is a history of ascetics living such disciplined and self-sufficient lives that their monasteries became wealthy—that wealth in turn bringing with it corruption, requiring renewed commitment to an ascetic life. There was, though, a deeper problem with the monastic life that

9. George W. Forell, ed., *Christian Social Teachings* (Minneapolis: Augsburg, 1971), 86–87.

was even harder to uproot. Waldo Beach describes it nicely, using
a metaphor drawn from academic life.

> The monastery was to be a lifelong "school of the Lord's ser-
> vice," where strict discipline and exactly prescribed "steps"
> might lead to the "commencement" of spiritual perfection. But
> in the curriculum of salvation the monk could easily become
> more concerned with his relation to the discipline than to the
> end for which the discipline was set, or, to speak by analogy,
> more concerned about getting grades than wisdom. . . . The self-
> denying charity of the monk to his indigent neighbor became,
> in much practice, a work of perfection, a sort of merit badge,
> so that the very self he struggled to deny remained at the center
> of his focus.[10]

To free us from a problem that deep-seated—which is more than
just a problem of possessions—another sort of deliverance is
needed. "You know," St. Paul wrote to the Corinthians, "the
grace of our Lord Jesus Christ, that though he was rich, yet
for your sake he became poor, so that by his poverty you might
become rich" (2 Cor. 8:9).

If we take seriously the commandments that forbid stealing
and coveting, we will not overlook or forget this deliverance. "You
have a rich Lord," Luther reminds us in his Large Catechism;
he "is surely sufficient for your needs."[11] Certainly we should
enjoy the many gifts God gives us through our possessions; yet,
it is all too easy to value those possessions mostly as a defense
against chance. All too easy, that is, to look to them for our
security—to grasp at them rather than receive them. The image
of the floating islands in C. S. Lewis's space fantasy *Perelandra*
pictures these alternative attitudes toward things. Perelandra is

10. Waldo Beach and H. Richard Niebuhr, eds., *Christian Ethics: Sources of
the Living Tradition*, 2nd ed. (New York: Ronald Press Company, 1973), 149–50.
11. Kolb and Wengert, *Book of Concord*, 450.

for the most part a world of floating islands, though it also has a Fixed Land. We need only try to picture such a world in order to be struck by the difference.

If we live on floating islands, it is beyond our power to say where we will be or what we will have near us from one day to the next. All we can do is learn to receive the gifts that are given with each new day. And we can understand how living that way might make us insecure and uneasy. Perelandra, as Lewis depicts it, is a newly created and unfallen world. Its only inhabitants, so far as we know, are a Lady and the King, though the story revolves almost entirely around the Lady. She is permitted to go onto the Fixed Land but forbidden to sleep there or live there. She has to live on the floating islands, which means that she cannot really secure her life from one day to the next, nor be certain that she and the King will not be separated. She accepts this, realizing that to want to live permanently on the Fixed Land would be "as if you gathered fruits together to-day for tomorrow's eating instead of taking what came."[12]

And that, of course, calls to mind the manna by which God feeds the Israelites in the wilderness. Moses' instructions to the people of Israel (in Exod. 16) are clear. Each morning they are to gather as much as they need and can eat for that day (except on the sixth day, when they may gather twice as much, in order to rest on the Sabbath). If they gather more than is needed—a little security against hunger the next day—it will spoil. Gathering extra manna, just like living on the Fixed Land, is a way of trying to secure our lives, a way of trusting more in our possessions than in the God who gives them.

Of course, how best to understand this lesson is not obvious. Although we have been reconciled to God in Christ, the creation is not yet redeemed and made new. In this sort of world we may

12. C. S. Lewis, *Perelandra* (New York: Macmillan, 1965), 208.

often need possessions. We need them because others are dependent on us for help and support. We need them lest we should
unduly burden others who have to care for us. We need them
because, in a world that still strains toward the promised new
creation, human life is often best structured when each of us has
possessions that enable us—in part—to see to our own needs. We
need them in order to live the sort of life St. Paul recommended
to the Corinthians—a life in which each of us has enough to look
to the needs of others. And we need them because a life marked
only by renunciation and not also by enjoyment fails to see that
our world remains God's good creation even when it is scarred
and disordered by sin.

Some of us—and perhaps especially those who warn against
inordinate love of possessions—also need to be reminded that
there is more than one way to go wrong in our desire for things.
As St. Thomas reminds us, we may want relatively few things
but want them in the wrong way. So, for example, I could simply eat too much, far more than I need. But I could also eat a
moderate amount while eating in a manner that insists on only
the best or most costly food in terms of its quality.[13] Similarly,
C. S. Lewis notes how a commitment, simply for its own sake,
to what we think of as high culture may be a distorted love of
created goods: "After a certain kind of sherry party, where there
have been cataracts of *culture* but never one word or one glance
that suggested a real enjoyment of any art, any person, or any
natural object, my heart warms to the schoolboy on the bus who
is reading *Fantasy and Science Fiction*, rapt and oblivious of all
the world beside. . . . Those who have greatly cared for any book
whatever may possibly come to care, some day, for good books.
The organs of appreciation exist in them."[14] Thus, there are

13. *Summa Theologiae* IIaIIae, q. 148, a. 4.
14. C. S. Lewis, *The World's Last Night and Other Essays* (New York: Harcourt
Brace Jovanovich, 1960), 39.

many different ways in which an inordinate love of things can take possession of our desires and lead us astray.

In this sinful but reconciled world we must try to live the life the Creator intended for us, a life marked by both enjoyment and renunciation of possessions. Probably, though, in a sinful world the need for renunciation becomes more pronounced—both because of the unmet needs of others and because our hearts too easily seek security in the things we have. We may pray to be given our daily bread, but the truth is we want manna for more than one day, and we would like to live on a Fixed Land. There is no cookbook recipe for how best to live—here and now—a life marked by both enjoyment and renunciation of possessions, nor is there a single path that all of us should follow. But each of us, in ways that suit our condition, must learn to control that desire for possessions, lest we should lose the capacity for trust.

The Possessions Bond and the Promised Redemption

A reader of the Decalogue looking for instruction about the proper attitude toward possessions would quickly take note of the commandments that prohibit stealing and coveting. But the commandment that, more than any other, ought to shape our attitude toward things is the injunction to keep the Sabbath day holy. In some respects this commandment is a puzzle for Christians, since few of them observe the Sabbath—the seventh day of the week—as a day of rest. We might suppose that they have simply transferred their Sabbath observance from the seventh day of the week to the first, and, indeed, that is the approach some Christians have taken.

But it is not the way Christian attitudes first developed. We can see from the New Testament that followers of Jesus, after his resurrection, began to observe the first day of the week as "the

Lord's day," a time for distinctively Christian worship.[15] That day
has its own special character, celebrating not just the Creator's
work but also Jesus' resurrection from the grave. In his *Brief
History of Sunday* Justo González notes the lack of evidence
in early Christian literature for the notion that "the Christian
Lord's day has taken the place of the Sabbath." Moreover, in that
literature "there is no expectation that on the Lord's day one is
to rest from one's labors, and to devote all the time to prayer,
meditation, and the study of Scripture."[16] It seems, in fact, that
many of the first Jewish Christians observed the Sabbath on
the seventh day and the Lord's day on the first day of the week.
Sunday worship did not replace the Sabbath but was "a separate
celebration of the resurrection of Jesus."[17]

That celebration has its own special, twofold character. As
the Sabbath command in Exodus (20:11) is grounded in God's
work of creation, so on Sunday we remember to look upon and
give thanks for the creation as "good." "There can," Josef Pieper
writes, "be no more radical assent to the world than the praise
of God, the lauding of the Creator of this same world."[18] Every
week the Lord's day breaks into the rhythms of work and everyday life, reminding us that our life and all life continually depends
on God and inviting us to offer back to God with thankful hearts
the whole creation. But just as the Sabbath command in Deuteronomy (5:15) is grounded in the great deliverance of Israel from
bondage in Egypt, so also on Sunday we look forward to the day
when, redeemed from "its bondage to decay," the entire creation
will "obtain the glorious liberty of the children of God" (Rom.
8:21). "It is impossible," Patrick Miller notes, "for Christians to

15. Cf. Rev. 1:10; Acts 20:7; 1 Cor. 16:2.
16. Justo L. González, *A Brief History of Sunday: From the New Testament to
the New Creation* (Grand Rapids: Eerdmans, 2017), 39.
17. González, *Brief History of Sunday*, 23.
18. Josef Pieper, *In Tune with the World: A Theory of Festivity* (South Bend,
IN: St. Augustine's Press, 1999), 31.

keep the Sabbath under the motivations provided by the Deu-
teronomic form of the commandment and not celebrate the first
day of the week. That is the day of remembering what God has
done for us, both when we were in slavery in Egypt and in our
slavery to sin and guilt."[19]

The promise of a new creation is the reason Christians have
felt free to treat each Sunday as a little Easter. Because Jesus was
truly "lord of the sabbath," they were free to set aside the cultic
requirements attached to the Sabbath, while observing the Lord's
day with praise for the goodness of creation and thanksgiving
for the promise of a redeemed creation.[20] Turning to Jesus' own
prayer book, they could apply the psalmist's words to Sunday:
"This is the day which the LORD has made; / let us rejoice and
be glad in it" (Ps. 118:24).

Nevertheless, Christians can learn something about how best
to celebrate Sunday by considering the meaning of the Sabbath
for Jews. In his profound discussion of the Sabbath, Rabbi Abraham Joshua Heschel notes how it directs our attention away
from space and toward time. "The portion of space which my
body occupies is taken up by myself in exclusion of anyone else.
Yet, no one possesses time. There is no moment which I possess
exclusively. . . . We share time, we own space."[21] Likewise, the
church's worship Sunday after Sunday, though it is rest from
the everyday world of work, is not at all the kind of rest that a
"vacation" involves. Vacations are taken by individuals and are
made possible by the things we possess; Sunday worship, by
contrast, is the activity of the people of God gathered together.
It is shared time—set aside for bringing the things we possess
and offering them back to the God who gives them. Michael

19. Miller, *Ten Commandments*, 164.
20. Matt. 12:8; Col. 2:16–17.
21. Abraham Joshua Heschel, *The Sabbath: Its Meaning for Modern Man* (New
York: Farrar, Straus and Giroux, 1951), 99.

Walzer notes that "in ancient Rome, the days on which there were
no religious festivals or public games were called *dies vacantes*,
'empty days.'"[22] But Sunday for Christians, like the Sabbath for
Jews, should be full—filled with shared celebration and marked
by trust that we are free from the need to secure our own life
through the things we possess.

Because the Sabbath is a cathedral built not in space but in
time, because on the Sabbath Jews set aside everyday work, it
serves, Heschel says, as a reminder that the world "will survive
without the help of man."[23] It serves to free us from our fear of
time's relentless progress, reminding us that we can and should
trust God to care for us. Even before the LORD spoke to Israel at
Sinai, the gift of manna to Israel in the wilderness had taught
this lesson. Likewise, when, together on the Lord's day, we pray
that God would give us *this day* the bread we need, we are trusting that the One whom we gather to worship every Sunday can
sustain us. He will do that through the hands of others, even as in
turn he uses our hands and our possessions to meet their needs.

There is one sense, though, in which the church's worship
is free to reclaim the world of things. Israel's Lord was not to
be depicted by means of the things of this world—that is, in
images. That Lord could not be located and confined in space;
he revealed himself not in a form or a shape but in a voice.
When Israel stands on the brink of entering the promised land,
Moses reminds them that "the LORD spoke to you out of the
midst of the fire; you heard the sound of words, but saw no
form; there was only a voice" (Deut. 4:12). But, as the writer
of Hebrews reminds us, when "today" we hear that voice, it
has a body—the body of "Jesus, the apostle and high priest of
our confession, . . . [who] was faithful to him who appointed

---

22. Michael Walzer, *Spheres of Justice* (New York: Basic Books, 1983), 194.
23. Heschel, *Sabbath*, 13.

him" (Heb. 3:1–2). We should, therefore, sanctify the world of things, using their beauty to honor the God who has shared our embodied life. Even so, however, we still look and long for a redeemed creation: "There remains a sabbath rest for the people of God" (4:9).

"Let us therefore," the author of Hebrews writes, "strive to enter that rest" (4:11). When the church gathers week after week for worship on the Lord's day, it recalls the work of creation and the beginning of a new creation in the risen Jesus—but also the promise of an "eighth day." The notion of an eighth day, common in the history of the church, has its origin in the Bible's creation story. If God began to create on the first day of the week and rested from that work on the seventh, then the first day of the week that follows would also be the eighth day. "In other words, the first day of the week, in which Christians celebrate the resurrection of Jesus, is also the eighth day, and therefore points to the final day of eternal joy and rest."[24]

On that day we will hear the promise hidden in God's commands. You *shall* not steal. You *shall* not covet. That rich Lord, who is sufficient for our needs, will see to it that we lack nothing. This is the eighth day of which St. Augustine speaks in the closing paragraphs of his *City of God*. A redeemed history will culminate in "our Sabbath, whose end will not be an evening, but the Lord's Day, an eighth day, . . . a day consecrated by the resurrection of Christ. . . . There we shall be still and see; we shall see and we shall love; we shall love and we shall praise."[25]

24. González, *Brief History of Sunday*, 29.

25. St. Augustine, *The City of God*, trans. Henry Bettenson (New York: Penguin, 1984), 22.30.

❧ CHAPTER 6 ❧

The Speech Bond

You shall not bear false witness against your neighbor.
You shall not take the name of the LORD your God in vain.

Exodus 20:16, 7

In one of the great penitential psalms, which has regularly made
its way into the church's worship, we pray: "O Lord, open thou
my lips, / and my mouth shall show forth thy praise" (Ps. 51:15).
And, in fact, once we begin to pay attention to the Psalms, we
will realize how often a similar theme is sounded. "My mouth is
filled with thy praise, / and with thy glory all the day" (71:8). "I
will bless the LORD at all times; / his praise shall continually be
in my mouth" (34:1). "It is good to give thanks to the LORD, / to
sing praises to thy name, O Most High" (92:1). Moreover, this
individual praise is to swell into a great chorus of voices. "My
mouth will speak the praise of the LORD, / and let all flesh bless
his holy name for ever and ever" (145:21). "Praise the LORD, all
nations! / Extol him, all peoples" (117:1). The goal toward which

all human speech is, in the end, directed is the praise of God, and that is at the heart of truthful speech.

Were our speech really truthful in that sense, it would not only direct us toward God but also bind human lives together in community. In our marriages and families our lives are bound together with near neighbors in love and friendship. We are also bound to more distant neighbors in the life we share, in the possessions we need to sustain that life, and—we can now add—through speech, without which we could hardly imagine life together. Thus, the second and the eighth commandments, taken together, remind us that truthful speech with one another has its ultimate ground in truthful speech about God. When we name God in praise, we will be helped to build up our common life, not tear it apart.

We are a long way from that goal. As the Letter of James reminds us, "the tongue is a fire . . . full of deadly poison" (3:6, 8). Because it is, truthful speech does not always come easily or naturally to us. Because truthful speech is needed to bind our lives together, the commandments set before us a task. Unsurprisingly, therefore, as the Psalms call us to praise, they also call us to discipline the fire of the tongue. "Set a guard over my mouth, O LORD, / keep watch over the door of my lips" (141:3).

The Speech Bond in Creation

Although the commandment forbidding false witness has usually been interpreted more broadly, it applies most directly to the legal and judicial systems. And clearly, a shared life in community could hardly be sustained if we were not willing to hold accountable those who perjure themselves in legal proceedings or, more generally, bear false witness against others in our public life. And in this public context we can see a connection between

the commandment forbidding false witness and the commandment forbidding the use of God's name in vain. To lie under
oath is not just a moral or legal wrong; it is also a religious offense. It certainly injures the person(s) about whom we lie, and
it undermines the bond of truthfulness a society needs, but, still
more, it seeks the support of God for the web of deceit we spin.

Invoking the name of God as warrant for our false speech, we
cozy up to the One who is truth itself in order to make our pursuit
of falsehood more effective. As Karl Barth put it, a liar "kisses
his Master as Judas did in Gethsemane."[1] He presents himself
publicly as affirming, not evading, the truth; he "confesses the
truth with the greatest emphasis and solemnity."[2] In this sense,
false testimony that invokes the name of God is especially dan-
gerous for Christians. Knowing Jesus as the One whom Barth
calls "the true witness," we should know that the two tables
of the law cannot neatly be severed, the eighth commandment
separated from the second. Evasion of the truth is for us evasion
of the One who is himself Truth (John 14:6). "Jesus Christ has
not yet met all men. Not every man as yet exists in direct and
immediate historical relation with Him." But for Christians who
do, "falsehood reach[es] maturity."[3]

This does not mean that only those who, like Jews and Christians, have been instructed by biblical teaching can know that
lying and deception are generally wrong. Insight into the structure
of human life as created by God is not the private possession of
religious believers. "Falsehood is in itself base and reprehensible,"
as Aristotle already knew, "and truth noble and praiseworthy."[4]
We need not doubt, therefore, that human beings are capable of

1. Karl Barth, *Church Dogmatics* IV/3, first half, ed. G. W. Bromiley and T. F.
Torrance, trans. G. W. Bromiley (Edinburgh: T&T Clark, 1961), 436.
2. Barth, *Church Dogmatics* IV/3, 437.
3. Barth, *Church Dogmatics* IV/3, 451.
4. Aristotle, *The Nicomachean Ethics*, Loeb Classical Library (Cambridge, MA:
Harvard University Press, 1947), 4.7.6.

some insight into what may be called the natural law, insight into the dangers of lying and the nobility of truth-telling.

Without the spoken word there can be no life together, and without truthful speech there can be no lasting or peaceful life together. One of the things any society needs is a capacity for making agreements on which everyone can rely. And unless we are able, at least most of the time, to trust the speech of those with whom we make such agreements, we are unlikely to be able to hold our common life together over time. No community can sustain itself indefinitely if its members cannot rely on each other to speak straightforwardly and truthfully; that is simply a necessity built into the nature of life in community.

Why this should be the case becomes clear when we remind ourselves that lying involves two different sorts of moral failure. On the one hand, it offends against the good of truth; for, turning against one of the created purposes of speech, the liar thinks one thing and deliberately says another. And on the other hand, it offends against the good of trust, undermining our readiness to take others at their word.

Something hangs on our judgment about which of these two offenses—against truth and against trust—is worse. If the real evil lies simply in false speech, in saying one thing while thinking another, there may still be plenty of room for deceiving others so long as we do not actually speak falsely. After all, we may speak truly even while counting on the listener to misunderstand what we mean and, hence, be deceived. Our speech may often be both technically true and intended to deceive. If, however, the more serious evil lies in the offense against trust, the prohibition of false speaking will cut more deeply into our purposes. Then it will not be enough to speak in ways that are technically true; rather, it will be wrong to try to manipulate and take control of words, using them for our own deceptive purposes. That kind of speech will surely undermine trust.

The Creator has so ordered human life that our societies cannot easily survive without at least a general commitment to truthful speech. Were lying a common and expected practice, it could easily turn out to be self-defeating; we could never trust each other. We would always wonder whether others were being truthful in their dealings with us, even as they would be likely to wonder about us. That is hardly a recipe for a flourishing communal life.

To be sure, this truth about the created world may not be apparent to us without some experience and instruction. Truth-telling does not always look like the way to get along with others. We may, on any given occasion, find that lying gets us out of a difficult situation and eases our relationship with someone else. But the larger community cannot sustain its shared life if such behavior becomes the common practice of many. We might rework sentences Peter Geach once wrote, substituting "truthfulness" for the virtues of courage and justice that he used to make his point. "Men need virtues as bees need stings. An individual bee may perish by stinging, all the same bees need stings; an individual man may perish by being truthful, all the same men need truthfulness."[5]

True as this is, it does not say everything that needs to be said on this subject. It does not seem to capture fully what Aristotle meant when he characterized falsehood as "base" and truth as "noble"—wholly apart, it would seem, from whether or not truthful speech can be calculated to help a society survive. For, after all, nobility might well be displayed in a refusal to deviate from the truth even at great cost to oneself or one's community. Therefore, if we penetrate more deeply into the

---

5. Geach's original sentences read as follows: "Men need virtues as bees need stings. An individual bee may perish by stinging, all the same bees need stings; an individual man may perish by being brave or just, all the same men need courage and justice" (Geach, *The Virtues* [London: Cambridge University Press, 1977], 17).

meaning of speech, we will think of truthful speech as something more than a recipe for communal survival. We will see
that the capacity for truthful speech is part of the grandeur
of our created nature. This is what human beings at their very
best are like—looking up to, praising, and honoring the One
who is Truth itself.

Seeing false speech as an offense against trust makes clear
that lying may be self-defeating. Remembering that lying is also
an offense against truth should remind us that it may be self-
corrupting. The problem with lying is not only what it does to
those whom we deceive but also what we do to ourselves. We can
gradually become people who are willing to take control of the
gift of speech—a gift intended to foster human community—
and use it to advance our private purposes. Thus, a willingness
to lie on some occasions always threatens to turn us into people
who are, simply, liars.

Of course, we may not always be certain what it means to
speak the truth or to lie. For example, Aquinas divides lies into
three kinds: officious (told to help another person), jocose (told
to please another), and mischievous (told for the sake of injuring
another).[6] Some of these are clearly worse than others, and some
should probably not be considered lies at all. A joke, for example,
would be a jocose lie according to St. Thomas's classification.
He would regard it as a lie, though far less grave than some other
lies. It makes more sense, however, not to regard it as a lie at all.
It is simply a form of communication that is intended to please
but does so by speaking in ways that are ambiguous or deceptive.
It does not seem to undermine our created capacity for truthful
speech; indeed, it depends on that capacity even as it playfully
subverts it. Or, to take a rather different example, when meeting
someone I might say, "How are you?" He might answer, "Just

6. *Summa Theologiae* IIaIIae, q. 110, a. 2.

fine, thank you," even though he has not been well for the last few days. That is not a lie. We all understand that these sorts of exchanges are not intended to convey accurate information about someone's health. They are simply pleasantries that serve to enable social interaction and, in fact, serve to demonstrate respect for those with whom we speak.

Moreover, since truthful speech is to bind us together, we always have to remind ourselves that actually communicating truth to another person is not just a matter of the words we speak. Just because someone can understand the words we speak does not mean that he or she is actually ready at any and every moment to hear the truth. Blunt statement of the facts—with respect to death, for example—is not necessarily truth-telling. On the one hand, the truth that I am dying should not simply be concealed from me. But on the other hand, it has to be communicated in a way that I can actually take it in and understand it. William F. May captures this nicely when he suggests that we need to honor

> the distance that the patient chooses to maintain in his or her relationship to the event. A man who knew that he had cancer once said to his middle-aged son, a writer on the subject of death and dying, "Go easy, Don." The man knew he had cancer. But at the same time he wanted to establish the distance he wished to maintain between himself, his son, and the imminent event of his death. . . . Only a fool would not have respected this request.[7]

Knowing that we are approaching the moment of our death is a truth not necessarily accessible to us at every moment. And communicating it to one who is dying is not simply a matter of

---

7. William F. May, *The Physician's Covenant*, 2nd ed. (Louisville: Westminster John Knox, 2000), 177–78.

using words that truly reflect the situation. The same is true of other kinds of information that cut very deeply into our sense of self—about what it means that we are sexual beings, for example. It should hardly surprise us that parents often struggle to convey that information to their children. If they do not say everything there is to be said all at once, they are not necessarily speaking untruthfully. They are beginning a process that they hope will neither move too quickly nor end prematurely. Here again, truthful speech is much more than just speaking words that mirror our thoughts.

It may also be hard sometimes to know whether one to whom we are speaking is entitled to know certain truths. Hence, the *Catechism of the Catholic Church* says quite directly, "No one is bound to reveal the truth to someone who does not have the right to know it."[8] How to respond in such circumstances can, of course, be very hard to determine. There may be instances in which it would be right to speak falsely—a possibility I take up below. But silence is also always an option, even if not always a very satisfactory one. And, of course, one can fall short of what the commandment requires even when telling the truth. For if we tell the truth but tell it in such a way and at such a time that others are harmed, we have not used the gift of speech in a way that binds human lives together.

Despite such complexities, the point of the second and eighth commandments should surely be clear to us. Human beings are

8. *Catechism of the Catholic Church* (Mahwah, NJ: Paulist Press, 1994), par. 2489. There are some complications, however. The first edition of the *Catechism*, which I cite here, described lying (in par. 2483) as follows: "To lie is to speak or act against the truth in order to lead into error someone who has the right to know the truth." In the revised, second edition this sentence reads: "To lie is to speak or act against the truth in order to lead someone into error." The point of the revision seems to be that, whereas the first formulation could be read to permit "lying" to one who has no right to know the truth, the revised formulation seems only to permit withholding information from a person who has no right to know the truth.

animals who speak. Through that created capacity our lives are bound together in community; with that created capacity we ought to honor and praise the God who gives it. Committed to truthful speech, we can pray sincerely, "Hallowed be thy name."

The Speech Bond in Need of Healing

Understanding our capacity for speech as a gift of the Creator, we can see why some of the greatest Christian thinkers—Augustine and Aquinas, for example—have viewed all lies, even relatively insignificant ones, as sinful. To think one thing while deliberately saying another, speaking in a way that places barriers between us and other people, subverts the purpose of the created gift of speech.

We need, however, to view the speech bond not only within the light of creation but also within the light of the need for healing in a sinful world. After all, we no longer live in Paradise. Several well-known stories in the Bible have always raised difficulties for those who want to condemn every instance of lying. Most well known, perhaps, is the story of the two Hebrew midwives who were charged by the Egyptian ruler to kill male children born to Hebrew women. As Exodus reports, "the midwives feared God, and did not do as the king of Egypt commanded them" (Exod. 1:17). Nor did they merely disobey the order. When asked to account for their action, the midwives said that the Hebrew women gave birth so quickly, after such a brief time in labor, that their children were already born before the midwives could arrive. "So God dealt well with the midwives," the biblical narrative reports, "and because the midwives feared God he gave them families" (1:20–21). Evidently the God-fearing character of those midwives was demonstrated in part by their willingness to lie to the Egyptian ruler. Also well known is the story (in Joshua chapter 2) of the prostitute Rahab in Jericho, who hid the Israelite spies and then lied when questioned concerning their whereabouts. When, later, Israel took the city of Jericho and destroyed it, Joshua specifically ordered that Rahab and her family be spared. And, we're told, "she dwelt in Israel to this day, because she hid the messengers whom Joshua sent to spy out Jericho" (Josh. 6:25).

Stories like these should make us wonder whether a blanket condemnation of lying may overlook important distinctions. For thinkers like Augustine and Aquinas, and many since who have agreed with them, a condemnation of all lies depends on a particular belief about the nature of language. As I character-ized it earlier, for those who hold this view it is always wrong to think one thing but say another. The sole purpose of speech, it seems, is to communicate our thoughts. Can such a view really be adequate? There are, after all, ways of speaking whose pur-pose is not to communicate what we are thinking. Quite often we use speech to encourage and comfort others, or, to take a very different sort of case, as a weapon to protect people who are weak and vulnerable. If we do not think that use of force to protect those who are innocent and defenseless violates the fifth commandment, why should we think that using false words as the weapon for defense violates the eighth?

Moreover, suppose we believe that untruthful speech is wrong just because what we say does not mirror what we think. Notice, then, how much room this view leaves for deception. Evidently it is perfectly fine to deceive others so long as the words we speak are technically true—so long as, that is, they truly re-flect what we are thinking. This seems to miss the point of the commandment, which is not just to make sure that we speak truly, but to use speech in order to bind human lives together harmoniously. If I speak the truth, but do so with the intent of deceiving others, I am undermining rather than enhancing the bond between us. Perhaps, then, those Hebrew midwives really were God-fearing and there is good reason to defend Rahab's actions.

One place where both lying and deceit may sometimes be necessary in a world deeply distorted by sin is the realm of politics. It is, for example, hard to imagine police work that never makes use of deceptive sting operations or undercover investigations. It is hard to imagine diplomacy entirely free of deception or a world entirely free of the need for espionage. Of course, given that nation-states understand these necessities, we might say that they have entered into a mutual agreement that false speech and spying are to be expected; they are simply part of any serious engagement in the world of politics. And even if we do not ourselves carry out the needed police work or deceptive diplomacy, we still are glad to have the protection it offers.

Even if there are exceptional circumstances in which lying may be justified, and even if some lies may be unavoidable for those who govern, we should not too easily or eagerly make our peace with that sad fact—and that for two reasons.

First, we cannot deny that a price must be paid for participating in such necessary activities—and perhaps even for accepting the fact that others do so on our behalf. In John le Carré's novel *The Spy Who Came In from the Cold*, set in the period of the Cold War between the United States and the Soviet Union, a British agent, Alec Leamas, engages in an elaborate deception intended—or so he thinks—to make it appear that his East German counterpart, Hans-Dieter Mundt, is a double agent, working for Britain. So complex are the webs of deception, however, that in the end Leamas realizes that his own British superiors have been deceiving him, using him to protect Mundt, who really is a double agent. However necessary all this may have been in the political context, the story invites us to reflect upon the ways in which immersing ourselves in a world of lies may be self-corrupting. In the end, at any rate, Leamas comes in from the cold; he turns back just when he might have escaped East Germany and returned to Britain. No longer able to accept responsibility for the webs of deception in which he has been entangled, he turns back and is shot—free at last from a corruption so profound that he can no longer bear to live within it. Participating in a practice of untruthful and deceptive speech, even in a very good cause, always brings with it the danger of corruption, a danger not easily escaped.

A second and perhaps even more important reason not to make our peace too easily with seemingly necessary lies is this: If there were never instances in which we had to permit evil and injustice rather than lie to prevent it, we would be on our way to eliminating from Christian life the possibility of martyrdom. Yet, the church has always honored her martyrs. "*Martyrdom* is the supreme witness given to the truth of the faith; it means bearing witness even unto death."[9] As Pope John Paul II taught in the encyclical letter *Veritatis Splendor*, the truth that some acts are always forbidden, even in a good cause, is "confirmed in a particularly eloquent way by Christian martyrdom, which has always accompanied and continues to accompany the life of the Church even today."[10] It is at least possible, therefore, that life might present us with circumstances in which, rather than speak untruthfully, we would have to permit evil at least a temporary moment of triumph. Christians can do this—or, at least, hope we are strong enough to do it—only because we trust that God himself has taken responsibility for the evils we have to permit. But we cannot ask this of those who do not yet know what God has done in Christ; martyrdom is more than

9. *Catechism of the Catholic Church*, par. 2473.
10. Pope John Paul II, *The Splendor of Truth* (Boston: St. Paul Books & Media, 1993), par. 90.

the natural law demands of anyone. It is precisely in acknowledging the limits to our own responsibility for achieving good outcomes—acknowledging that we are not gods—that we open up space in life for martyrdom.

Clearly, the commandment forbidding false witness and enjoining truthful speech has many complications of the sort discussed here, and they can be difficult to sort out. But in the midst of those complexities we should not lose sight of the basic point. On the most straightforward reading, the commandment directs our attention to legal and judicial proceedings. And its concern is not simply that in such proceedings we should speak truthfully. The point is that these are occasions in which we are called to speak on behalf of others who have been mistreated and to defend the good name of those who need us to speak up on their behalf.

That was a special emphasis of the great Reformers, Luther and Calvin. This is clear in the simple explanation of the eighth commandment given in Luther's Small Catechism, where the negative prohibitions lead to positive commitments: "We are to fear and love God, so that we do not tell lies about our neighbors, betray or slander them, or destroy their reputations. Instead we are to come to their defense, speak well of them, and interpret everything they do in the best possible light."[11] Although Luther notes that public sin must be publicly rebuked, he emphasizes also in the Large Catechism that in all other instances we should "use our tongue to speak only the best about all people."[12] Calvin is, if anything, even more insistent. While also noting that public correction may sometimes be needed, he notes that most of us are all too eager to speak ill of others. "We delight in a certain

11. Robert Kolb and Timothy J. Wengert, eds., *The Book of Concord: The Confessions of the Evangelical Lutheran Church* (Minneapolis: Fortress, 2000), 353.
12. Kolb and Wengert, *Book of Concord*, 422.

poisoned sweetness experienced in ferreting out and in disclosing the evils of others. And let us not think it an adequate excuse if in many instances we are not lying."[13]

Clearly, the central teaching of the commandment is its call to truthful speech. Even in a world broken and distorted by sin, following Jesus who is the way, the *truth*, and the life means far more than avoiding lying and duplicity. It means knowing when to speak and when to be silent. It means bearing witness to the truth, even if at some cost to oneself. It means, as Luther says, using the spoken word to come to the defense of others and to speak well of them.

The Speech Bond and the Promised Redemption

Joachim Jeremias characterized the Sermon on the Mount (in Matt. 5–7) as "an early Christian Catechism."[14] Distinguishing kerygma (preaching) from didache (teaching), he wrote, "The Sermon on the Mount as a whole is, together with the Epistle of James, the classical example of an early Christian didache."[15] We should, therefore, pay attention to what Jesus says in the Sermon about truthfulness in our speech. His words there are well known: "Let what you say be simply 'Yes' or 'No'; anything more than this comes from evil" (Matt. 5:37). Taken in its immediate context, this verse seems to go well beyond what is proscribed in the second or the eighth commandment. As Patrick Miller notes, "Swearing an oath by the Lord's name is what Deuteronomy 6:13 presents as a positive form" of the commandment

13. John Calvin, *Institutes of the Christian Religion*, ed. John T. McNeill, trans. Ford Lewis Battles, Library of Christian Classics 20 (Philadelphia: Westminster, 1960), 2.8.48.

14. Joachim Jeremias, *The Sermon on the Mount* (Philadelphia: Fortress, 1963), 19.

15. Jeremias, *Sermon on the Mount*, 22.

that prohibits misuse of the name of God. Hence, the commandment could not have been understood to prohibit all swearing of oaths.[16] Yet, Jesus not only condemns *false* witness against one's neighbor or a *vain* use of God's name, he seems to forbid oath-taking entirely and, presumably also, participation in judicial functions that require it. In an earlier time, Jesus says, Israelites were forbidden to swear falsely, but now "I say to you, Do not swear at all" (Matt. 5:34).

It is obvious—and easily noted—that almost from the start, Christians did not seem to observe this prohibition strictly.[17] "Men indeed swear by a greater than themselves, and in all their disputes an oath is final for confirmation" is a truism evidently accepted by the writer of Hebrews (6:16). And St. Paul himself does not hesitate more than once to call God as "witness" to the truth of his words.[18] Especially if the good name and reputation of another is at stake, we need not draw back even from an oath if it is needed. That too can be a way of following Jesus, who is not only the "way" and the "life," but also the "truth."[19] As his Spirit shapes and reshapes our character, we can begin to become people who genuinely want what is good for our neighbors. When and as we do, we can seek and find the truthful word that binds our lives together.

Nevertheless, the very need for oath-taking in our world should move us to hope for a world in which oath-taking is unnecessary. For an oath is something more than just a vow or a promise in which we commit ourselves to do something or to

16. Patrick D. Miller, *The Ten Commandments* (Louisville: Westminster John Knox, 2009), 69.

17. But this is not always the case. Cf. James 5:12, which directly echoes Jesus' words in the Sermon on the Mount: "But above all, my brethren, do not swear, either by heaven or by earth or with any other oath, but let your yes be yes and your no be no, that you may not fall under condemnation."

18. Rom. 1:9; 2 Cor. 1:23.

19. John 14:6.

act in a certain way. In an oath we call on God to stand behind and confirm our speaking, to act as guarantor not just of what is said but of the one who says it. Therefore, as Helmut Thielicke noted, "the oath demands not merely that I *do* something but that I *be* something, namely, a loyal person."[20]

In taking an oath, therefore, we reach out in longing for a redeemed world, a world made whole in which our word need not be doubted. Thus, the very act of taking an oath reminds us that the Christian life must be lived in hope in the promises of God. But, true as that is, we should not be content with a world in which broken promises and lies are accepted as a part of everyday life and considered all right so long as we live in hope for something better. We may defend the lies of the Hebrew midwives and Rahab. Indeed, we may believe that God defends them. This does not mean, however, that we should be content with a fractured world in which the tongue must sometimes be used to deceive rather than to praise. After all, what we hope for is that purity of heart which, as Jesus says, will "see God."[21]

The Spirit of the risen Christ draws us ever more fully into that resurrected life in which we—and, hence, our speech—will be healed and made whole. That kind of harmony between our inner desires and our outer words is only possible, however, in a world redeemed and made new; hence, we pray daily, "Thy kingdom come." In that redeemed creation the psalmist's words will truly characterize our lives: "I will bless the LORD at all times; / his praise shall continually be in my mouth" (Ps. 34:1). Nothing then will remain but praise.

Until that day, however, we will need to listen for the promise in the command. You *shall* not bear false witness against your

20. Helmut Thielicke, *Theological Ethics*, vol. 2, *Politics* (Philadelphia: Fortress, 1969), 380.
21. Matt. 5:8.

neighbor. You *shall* not take the name of the Lord your God in vain. You *shall* be people in whom the true purpose of speech is realized, people in whose speech the praise of God resounds. One day we shall be such truthful people, for the One who is Truth itself is committed to making us whole.

CHAPTER 7

The Great and
First Commandment

You shall have no other gods before me.

Exodus 20:3

You shall love the Lord your God with all your heart, and with all your soul, and with all your mind. This is the great and first commandment. And a second is like it, You shall love your neighbor as yourself.

Matthew 22:37–39

The commandments of the Decalogue direct our attention to the most significant ways in which human lives are bound together—in families, in marriages, in the gift of life we share, in the possessions that connect our lives in countless ways, and in the spoken word that makes life in community possible. It would be difficult to exaggerate the richness these bonds add to life or the importance they have for us.

And yet, the first commandment exists to remind us that, important as they are, they cannot have first place in our hearts. If we try to make them everything, they will disappoint us in the end. The Decalogue is clear that God must come first. But Jesus' statement of "the great and first commandment," like that of Moses to Israel in Deuteronomy (6:4–5), seems even stronger. It is not just that we are to love God first, ahead of our other loves; it is that we are to love God with "all" our heart, soul, and mind. What place in life does this leave for those other attachments that seem so integral to human happiness? There are, after all, two great commandments. How are we to hold together our natural human loves with the command to love God with all that we are? We cannot take the Decalogue seriously without reflecting on that question.

The First Commandment in the World God Created

When, shortly before his death, Joshua reminds Israel of the LORD's past dealings with them, he notes that their ancestors had worshiped other gods. "Your fathers lived of old beyond the Euphrates, Terah, the father of Abraham and of Nahor; and they served other gods" (Josh. 24:2).[1] This suggests that the first commandment is not primarily an affirmation of monotheism— the belief that there is only one God. Its claim, rather, is that the God who has covenanted with Israel "will not tolerate a divided loyalty."[2] And most often Israel's temptation was not turning from the LORD to worship other gods; rather, it was the temptation to

1. See also the mention in Gen. 35:2 of the various gods present in Jacob's household.
2. Brevard S. Childs, *Old Testament Theology in a Canonical Context* (Philadelphia: Fortress, 1985), 65. And in articulating the call for exclusive loyalty to the LORD, Moses does not precisely affirm monotheism. See Deut. 4:7, 34.

worship other gods "in addition" to the One who had set them free.[3] Jesus makes the same point in the Sermon on the Mount: "No one can serve two masters; for either he will hate the one and love the other, or he will be devoted to the one and despise the other. You cannot serve God and mammon" (Matt. 6:24).

Nevertheless, family and friends, life and possessions, all come to us as gifts of the Creator. They are instruments through which God cares for us and enriches human life. It would not be wrong, therefore, to say that Christian faith is worldly. We rightly love the things and people in our lives, but we must learn to think of them always in relation to God. They are vehicles through which the Creator's glory reaches us. Our love for every other good thing must be taken up into our love for God. Something like this is what Josef Pieper meant when he characterized the Christian understanding of the natural world as "theologically grounded worldliness."[4] The good things of our world are good precisely because they participate in the goodness of the Creator. The glory of God shines into our lives through them, directing our hearts and minds back to the One who is glory itself. It is no surprise, therefore, that God uses tangible, worldly things—the water of baptism, the bread and wine of the Eucharist—to grace our lives. But because our worldliness is theologically grounded, it might also be said to be otherworldly. Shafts of the divine glory strike us *through* others, but the glory is not *in* them or in the things we possess. So a theologically grounded worldliness means that we enjoy the good things of creation while—simultaneously—turning from them to the God who gives them. That is the nature of Christian life and love.

There are two great commandments. We are to love both God and the neighbor. When we love God, we are loving the One

3. David L. Baker, *The Decalogue: Living as the People of God* (Downers Grove, IL: IVP Academic, 2017), 43.

4. Josef Pieper, "The Christian West," *Commonweal* 2, March 15, 1957, 607.

who gives us neighbors to care for and love. When we love the neighbor, we are loving one who is God's gift to us. We must think them together and learn to love them together.

To say that we are to love the neighbor "in God" is, of course, a general statement that does not necessarily tell us much in particular about what we ought to do and say. But if we see the world as God's creation, if we expect to find God's will for human life embedded in it, we should expect that some insight into the right and the good will be available to us if we try to discern what sort of behavior really serves human flourishing and cares for the creation. That is, we should expect to find at least some insight into what we may call natural law. I have already noted several times earlier a minimal sense in which this is true. The five bonds to which the Decalogue points, bonds that connect our lives in important ways, play an essential role in the survival of our communities. If we ignore them or undermine them, life in society becomes difficult, even impossible. That kind of natural law, though not insignificant, is merely descriptive. It points to regularities in nature that simply go on around us, come what may.

But the natural law embedded in our world by the Creator points to something richer than just regularities in nature. In discerning this natural law we learn more than what is minimally necessary for our societies to survive; we learn what it means for them to flourish, what truly serves human well-being, what it would mean for us to live fully in accord with the Creator's will. So, to take just one instance, consider the family bond. Of course, it—or something like it—is needed if we are to sustain and perpetuate a common life in society. When, however, we discern the Creator's handiwork built into our life, we will see something richer: the family bond as a place of cooperation and connection, the place where we first begin to learn the meaning of love and grow into mature human beings.

Putting it this way, however, immediately suggests a complication. To come to know natural law in this richer sense requires something more than reason alone. If we are asking what it means to grow into mature human beings, we can hardly answer that question without reference to Jesus; for, as Ephesians (4:13) says, "the stature of the fulness of Christ" is the measure of mature humanity. "All things were made through him," as John's Gospel says.[5] The standard, then, is not what it might mean for a generic human being to flourish; the standard is this single individual, and, however strange it may seem, he is the measure of human flourishing.

We cannot, therefore, take the Decalogue seriously as the will of God for us without also attending to Jesus' restatement and sharpening of it in the Sermon on the Mount (Matt. 5–7). Honoring one's father and mother is essential; yet, not only near but also distant neighbors are to be loved. And even father and mother may not be rivals to our love for God. At the heart of the marriage bond is a faithfulness that may sometimes be called to go well beyond what seems to bring enjoyment or flourishing. Respect for the life of another means something far more demanding than simply refraining from harm. It requires that we seek peace with others. It calls for a kind of selflessness which, although willing to protect others against enemies who threaten them harm, does not do in our own defense what we do for others. The truthful speech Jesus asks of us goes well beyond keeping our promises and avoiding lying. We are to be people who can be trusted when we speak and when we refrain from speaking, people whose speech serves the needs of others and gives glory to God. And in its clear teaching that we cannot serve both God and mammon, the Sermon requires that we regularly ask ourselves what we really treasure in our heart, that we be people ready to give to others who are in need.

5. John 1:3. Cf. also Col. 1:16.

To whom, then, is the Sermon on the Mount directed? Not to the world generally, as if it were a law for governing our communities or an impossible ideal intended simply to demonstrate how far short of holiness we all are. Rather, it is spoken to those who are seeking Jesus and trying, however haltingly, to follow him. That is the setting into which Matthew places the Sermon. "Seeing the crowds, [Jesus] went up on the mountain, and when he sat down his disciples came to him. And he opened his mouth and taught them" (Matt. 5:1–2).

We must, however, immediately add that if the Sermon is spoken only to Jesus' disciples, it is spoken to all of them—to all who seek to follow him, not just to some. We should not distinguish between "garden-variety" Christians, who settle for trying to obey the Decalogue, and other Christians, who seek a perfection outlined in the Sermon but possible only for some few. The Sermon is Christian catechesis, directed to those who trust that in Jesus the Creator of this world has come to live among us.[6] To be sure, it "is not a complete regulation of the life of the disciples, and it is not intended to be; rather, what is here taught is symptoms, signs, examples of what it means when the kingdom of God breaks into the world."[7] All of Jesus' followers must struggle as best they can to discern the obedience to which he calls them in a world where they are his witnesses. Then they will be "like a wise man who built his house upon the rock," surviving the storms of life.[8]

The First Commandment in a Creation in Need of Healing

Reflecting on the fact that the first commandment is indeed first, Karl Barth observed, "All the laws of Israel and all the concrete

6. Joachim Jeremias, *The Sermon on the Mount* (Philadelphia: Fortress, 1963).
7. Jeremias, *Sermon on the Mount*, 33.
8. Matt. 7:24.

demands addressed by God to individual men in Israel are simply developments and specific forms of this one law, demands not to withhold from the God of the covenant the thanks which is His due but to render it with a whole heart."[9] Hence, as directed to Israel and now also to the church, the Decalogue outlines the shape of lives set free from bondage. In both Exodus (20:2) and Deuteronomy (5:6), the God who will allow no rivals identifies himself at the outset as Israel's deliverer: "I am the LORD your God, who brought you out of the land of Egypt, out of the house of bondage."[10]

Of course, as Israel's history and our own lives attest, to be set free is not yet to be healed and made whole. Human nature, Calvin notes, "is a perpetual factory of idols," and we are all too ready to fall back into slavery to one or another of them.[11] To love all things in God is not hard to say, but to live such love will sometimes call for renunciation even of the good gifts of creation. Hence, in a world still in need of healing, loving all things in God, serving not two masters but one, will often be experienced as painful.

Such renunciation was famously depicted by John Bunyan in *The Pilgrim's Progress.* When Christian begins to flee the City of Destruction, his wife and children call him to stop and come back. But, putting his fingers in his ears, he runs on, crying, "'Life! life! eternal life!' (Luke xiv, 26)."[12] In the passage from Luke 14 to which Bunyan refers parenthetically, Jesus says, "If any one comes to me and does not hate his own father and mother and

9. Karl Barth, *Church Dogmatics* IV/1, ed. G. W. Bromiley and T. F. Torrance (Edinburgh: T&T Clark, 1956), 42–43.

10. This emphasis is not confined to these two texts. See, e.g., Ps. 81:8–10.

11. John Calvin, *Institutes of the Christian Religion*, ed. John T. McNeill, trans. Ford Lewis Battles, Library of Christian Classics 20 (Philadelphia: Westminster, 1960), 1.11.8.

12. John Bunyan, *The Pilgrim's Progress* (London: J. M. Dent & Sons Ltd., 1907), 10.

wife and children and brothers and sisters, yes, and even his own life, he cannot be my disciple." There is surely something harsh in the image of Christian making himself deaf to the pleas of those most closely bound to him in love.[13] And no doubt there is a sense in which it is right to take Jesus' saying as exaggerated in order to make clear that love of God is the great and first commandment. The renunciation asked of us does not suggest that the many good gifts of creation are not truly good, are not really to be loved, and do not really bring pleasure. "Joy, pleasure, and merriment" the Creator has, as C. S. Lewis once put it, "scattered broadcast" in our lives.[14] But Jesus' clear statement of the renunciation that may be required does mean that, if we really face a choice between God and any of our other loves, God comes first. We may all hope not to face such moments in life.

In another sense, however, we might say that we face such choices at every moment in our lives. There are, after all, two great commandments—to love God above all else and to love the neighbor—and we must live these loves simultaneously. If it is easy, or even pleasant, for us to cover our ears and turn—as we suppose—toward God and away from those who love us, if we do not experience this as renunciation of a great good, then we are not really seeking or attempting simultaneity in our loves. Nor, then, do we even love God rightly, since it is God who gives us other people and other good things to love.

We should, therefore, think of the needed renunciation not solely, or even primarily, as a choice we face in rare and tension-filled moments. We should think of the Christian life as a series of smaller renunciations, day-by-day decisions in which we sacrifice

13. We should not forget, though, that *The Pilgrim's Progress* is an allegory. The pilgrim fleeing the City of Destruction does not represent all truths about the Christian life. He represents a wholehearted commitment that wills always to love God above all else.

14. C. S. Lewis, *The Problem of Pain* (New York: Macmillan, 1962), 115.

one or another of the goods given us in the five bonds of human life in order to live out our faithfulness to God. The needed renunciations will be different for each of us; here again there is no single recipe for the life of love, and only God knows what each of us needs. For some of us, it may be the powerful lure of possessions that threatens to draw us away from God. For some it may be the determination to defend ourselves through our actions or our speech that seems to take first place in our desires and affections. And for some it may be the bonds of marriage and family that occupy in our hearts the place that is to be God's alone, so quick are we to forget that these are earthly bonds, not the heart of the promised redeemed creation.

To commit ourselves to a life shaped *simultaneously* by both of the great love commands will remind us daily that we are in need of healing—and that a world which often seems to force us to choose between the Creator and his gifts to us is a world not yet fully redeemed. Luther described the character of such a life well in his Small Catechism, explaining the shape of the baptized life: Baptism signifies that "the old creature in us with all sins and evil desires is to be drowned and die through daily contrition and repentance, and on the other hand that daily a new person is to come forth and rise up to live before God in righteousness and purity forever."[15]

It is essential for us to see that all who are baptized into this new life, all who are committed to such daily contrition and repentance and to the attempt to live before God in righteousness and purity, are united in that new bond we call the church. It is not merely another voluntary organization that exists to serve the projects and purposes of the societies around it. On the contrary, the church has its own way of life, its own culture. That is what

15. Robert Kolb and Timothy J. Wengert, eds., *The Book of Concord: The Confessions of the Evangelical Lutheran Church* (Minneapolis: Fortress, 2000), 360.

Dietrich Bonhoeffer meant when he wrote, "The body of Christ takes up physical space here on earth."[16] Because the church has its own way of life, we cannot understand the bonds of life to which the Decalogue points only in terms of their created order. We must draw them into the entire history of redemption, which includes a creation now in need of healing and reconciliation, and the promise of a redeemed creation. Thus, as Robert Jenson once noted, the issue for us is not so much the relation between Christ and culture, "as if Christ were one sort of reality and culture simply another," but, instead, the relation between "Christ and Other Cultures."[17]

To take Jenson's point seriously is to understand that the deepest renunciation required of the baptized is renunciation of the secular culture within which the church exists. Whether that secular culture is friendly or hostile to the church makes no crucial difference at this point. In either case, the church does not exist as an organization whose reason for being is to serve the projects of the society in which it finds itself. On the contrary, the body of Christ takes up space on earth. The church needs no reason for being other than the simple fact that the risen and ascended Christ has established it as the place of his presence. So the church is not a disembodied set of ideas, teachings, or beliefs. The church is its own culture. It is a separate society, called out from the nations by the God of Israel, who took flesh in the crucified and risen Jesus of Nazareth. As David Yeago has put it very precisely, the church is "the present civic assembly of the eschatological city, constituting a new public order which occupies its own public space in the midst of the nations."[18]

16. Dietrich Bonhoeffer, *Discipleship*, ed. Geffrey B. Kelly and John D. Godsey, trans. Barbara Green and Reinhard Krauss, Dietrich Bonhoeffer Works 4 (Minneapolis: Fortress, 2001), 225.

17. Robert Jenson, "It's the Culture," *First Things* (May 2014), 35.

18. David S. Yeago, "Messiah's People: The Culture of the Church in the Midst of the Nations," *Pro Ecclesia* 6, no. 2 (Spring 1997): 148.

To be sure, the church does not exist in a separate space; it shares its space with various other cultures in which the baptized are found. Hence, though it has its own way of life, "the culture of the church is always involved in absorbing and transforming and reshaping elements of the cultures of the nations which its members, so to speak, bring with them."[19] That, again, is why we must view the bonds of life within the history of redemption, which includes not only their created nature but also their need for healing and the promise of a redeemed creation. Because the church has its own distinctive way of life, because it takes up its own space, we can never specify in advance what we may have to leave behind—to renounce—in order to share in the life of the body of Christ. To love God with all our heart, soul, and mind is to be called out into a future we cannot clearly see, knowing only that we are called to follow.

The First Commandment and the Promised Redemption

We do, though, know one truth about that future. Seeing in Jesus the face of the God who asks *all* that we are, we can be confident that the way of renunciation is not alien to God. In Jesus, God has been there ahead of us, making it possible for us to say, "His commandments are not burdensome."[20] What the first commandment means, as Luther says in his Large Catechism, is "See to it that you let me alone be your God, and never search for another."[21] What we cannot do for ourselves or make of ourselves, the Spirit of the risen Christ promises to do in us. Hence, there is place neither for despair nor presumption in the Christian life. We need not despair, because the path of obedience—and,

19. Yeago, "Messiah's People," 152.
20. 1 John 5:3.
21. Kolb and Wengert, *Book of Concord*, 387.

if need be, renunciation—is not alien to God. And we have no
reason for presumption, since we do no more than follow One
to whom we look for all that is good.[22]

This means that what we cannot, for now, see we are invited
to believe—namely, that whatever must be renounced for the
sake of loyalty to God will, in the end, not count as loss. In
that sense, Bunyan's pilgrim was not mistaken. And that is precisely the point of Luther's great Reformation hymn, "A Mighty
Fortress Is Our God." It directs our attention to the five ways
in which human lives are bound together, bonds to which the
Decalogue points.[23] Significant and enriching as these are, they
do not come first.

> Nehman sie den Leib,
> Gut, Ehr', Kind und Weib:
> Lass fahren dahin
> Sie haben's kein'n Gewinn,
> Das Reich muss uns doch bleiben.

> And take they our life,
> Goods, fame, child, and wife,
> Let these all be gone,
> They yet have nothing won;
> The Kingdom ours remaineth.

22. How infelicitous, however, is the following characterization of presumption
in the *Catechism of the Catholic Church* (Mahwah, NJ: Paulist Press, 1994), par.
2092: "There are two kinds of *presumption*. Either man presumes upon his own
capacities (hoping to be able to save himself without help from on high), or he
presumes upon God's almighty power or his mercy (hoping to obtain his forgiveness
without conversion and glory without merit)." While it may be possible to read
this passage in a way that is theologically adequate, it does not clearly distinguish
the forbidden presumption from a faith that trusts wholeheartedly in the God from
whom all good comes.

23. I quote the German here and an older English translation (from *The Lutheran
Hymnal* [St. Louis: Concordia, 1941]), because more recent translations have tended
to obscure the way in which the hymn directs our attention to these five bonds—
life, possessions, speech (and the reputation it may harm), family, and marriage.

We can say very little about what the redeemed life will be like, but we should be confident that we will then see what for now is often hidden from our sight: the promise buried in the commands. It is worth noting that when, in Romans 13:9, St. Paul cites some of the commandments of the Decalogue and the second great commandment as their summary, he uses not imperatives but future-tense verbs (though this is less apparent in English, where the difference is not obvious). "The commandments, 'You shall not commit adultery, You shall not kill, You shall not steal, You shall not covet,' and any other commandment, are summed up in this sentence, 'You shall love your neighbor as yourself.'"

In that day, in the promised new creation, the tension between the two great commandments will be no more. We will hear again the ten words, but now clearly as promise. You *shall* love the LORD your God with all your heart, soul, and mind. You *shall* be a bride eager to greet her bridegroom, a child who loves the Father, a creature who honors the life of every fellow human being, a creature whose Lord is rich enough to meet every need, a lover of God whose first and last word is, "Thy will be done."

Index